Charles Jennings studied n became, as reported in the S̶p̶e̶c̶t̶a̶t̶o̶r̶, the funniest journalist in London. He has written numerous books, including a history of Greenwich, as well as *Them and Us: The American Invasion of English High Society* (2007).

Recent titles in the series

A Brief Guide to the Supernatural
Leo Ruickbie

A Brief Guide to Star Trek
Brian J. Robb

Star Wars
The Unauthorised Inside Story of George Lucas's Epic
Brian J. Robb

A Brief Guide to Secret Religions
David Barrett

A Brief History of Angels and Demons
Sarah Bartlett

A Brief History of Bad Medicine
Robert Youngston

A Brief History of France
Cecil Jenkins

A Brief History of Slavery
Jeremy Black

A Brief History of Sherlock Holmes
Nigel Cawthorne

A Brief History of King Arthur
Mike Ashley

A Brief History of the Universe
J. P. McEvoy

A Brief History of Roman Britain
Joan P. Alcock

A Brief History of the Private Life of Elizabeth II
Michael Patterson

A BRIEF GUIDE TO

JANE AUSTEN

CHARLES JENNINGS

RUNNING PRESS
PHILADELPHIA · LONDON

ROBINSON

Constable & Robinson
55–56 Russell Square
London WC1B 4HP
www.constablerobinson.com

First published in the UK by Robinson,
An imprint of Constable & Robinson, 2012

A copy of the British Library Cataloguing in
Publication data is available from the British Library

ISBN 978-1-78033-046-4 (paperback)
ISBN 978-1-78033-047-1 (ebook)

1 3 5 7 9 10 8 6 4 2

First published in the United States in 2012 by Running Press Book Publishers,
A Member of the Perseus Books Group

Books published by Running Press are available at special discounts for bulk purchases in the United
States by corporations, institutions, and other organizations. For more information, please contact the
Special Markets Department at the Perseus Books Group, 2300 Chestnut Street, Suite 200,
Philadelphia, PA 19103, or call (800) 810-4145, ext. 5000, or email
special.markets@perseusbooks.com.

US ISBN 978-0-7624-4629-2
US Library of Congress Control Number: 2011942359

9 8 7 6 5 4 3 2 1
Digit on the right indicates the number of this printing

Running Press Book Publishers
2300 Chestnut Street
Philadelphia, PA 19103-4371

Visit us on the web!
www.runningpress.com

Typeset by TW Typesetting, Plymouth, Devon

Printed and bound in the UK

CONTENTS

Map		*vi*
Introduction		*viii*
1	**Jane Austen – The Life**	1
2	**Jane Austen – The Novels**	77
	Sense and Sensibility	77
	Pride and Prejudice	91
	Mansfield Park	102
	Emma	117
	Persuasion	132
	Northanger Abbey	143
3	**Jane Austen's Regency**	155
	The Regency	155
	I. The Home	162
	II. Dress	172
	III. Education and Accomplishments	179
	IV. The Day	186
	V. Meals	193
	VI. Pleasure	201
	VII. Manners	208
	VIII. Travel	212
	IX. Transport	216
	X. After the Regency	221
4	**After Jane**	224
Bibliography		*237*
Index		*239*

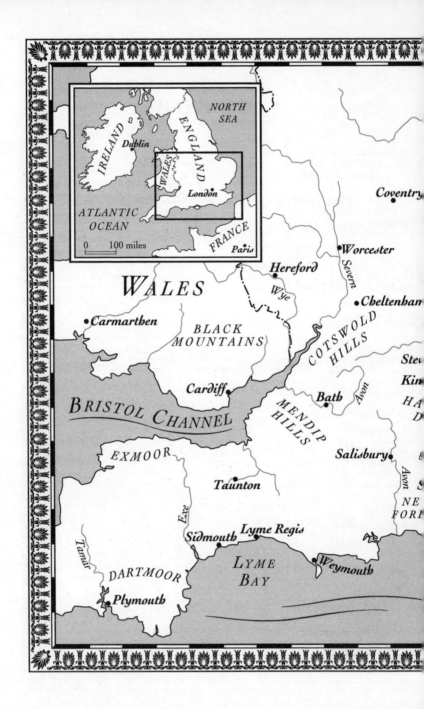

THE WASH

Norwich

N

Great Ouse

·thampton

·Cambridge

ENGLAND

Colchester

Oxford

CHILTERN HILLS

London

Thames

Reading

Rochester·

Stour

·Basingstoke

NORTH DOWNS

Goodnestone
·Park

HIRE

·Alton

Medway

Godmersham

·Chawton

Winchester

STRAITS OF DOVER

·mpton

SOUTH DOWNS

Brighton

·LE OF
IGHT

Portsmouth

ENGLISH CHANNEL

0   50   100 miles

INTRODUCTION

Jane Austen is so well-known, her novels so central to literary culture, why does one need a guide? After all, Mr Darcy, Emma Woodhouse, Mr Collins and Fanny Price are such familiar presences that we use them as conversational shorthands; while Pemberley has turned into a destination as fixed in the popular consciousness as Daphne du Maurier's fictional estate Manderley, or Evelyn Waugh's Brideshead. And everyone thinks they can recognize her prose when they see it, especially the opening lines of *Pride and Prejudice*.

But – for all her popularity, all her acknowledged genius – it's not as easy to dive straight into one of Jane Austen's novels as it is with the works of, say, Charles Dickens or Mark Twain. Her apparent modernity – her cool ironies, her sense of place, and her wit – can be misleading. The two hundred years between her society and ours are a real gap, and some sort of background is useful, however well we think we know the landscape. Miss Austen, too, needs introducing. Few writers are so well loved by their readerships; but why, exactly?

A Brief Guide examines Jane Austen from three angles. The biographical section is presented as its own narrative, in order to let the shape of her life emerge. After all, the great majority of it was spent in dependent spinsterhood, a very unconsidered existence. Only the last five years offered her the chance to become Jane Austen, the writer, and thus escape the condition that had until then defined her. Her success came late, and in a rush; and I want that shape to be clear. I'm also keen to avoid the dreaded biographical fallacy, of tying biographical events too closely to events and characters in the fiction. Physically separating the two seems a good way of keeping history and the creative imagination in their rightful places.

When talking about the novels, I've done my best to see them from the perspective of the interested contemporary reader, with no particular axe to grind. All the novels present problems, in one way or another, and I've tried to pick out the most important ones, the ones I think most likely to make the reader scratch his or her head. At the same time I've tried to identify the good bits, or at least the bits I think are good. Of course, it's possible to read just about anything into the works of Jane Austen, including proto-feminism, anti-slavery, problems with the cult of the Picturesque and a critique of the Monarchy. Great novels persistently lay themselves open to interpretations and re-interpretations, and Miss Austen's 'big six' are no different. But in *A Brief Guide* I'm less intrigued by the possibility of reading into *Sense and Sensibility* pretty much whatever you want to read into it, and more interested in the idea that Austen's novels are not perfect. There are wrong turns and mis-steps, and the best way to

approach her is with a degree of critical caution, acknow-
ledging the fallibilities, and seeing how often she triumphs
over them.

The Regency section explains itself – a compressed
attempt to paint in the social background, answering, along
the way, such questions as: what time was dinner, and how
many courses were there; how often did people wash; why
was Brighton considered so louche; and why does Emma
not call Mr Knightley by his first name? Questions, in
other words, that might easily come up in the course of
reading.

One of the very best ways to spend your time is in
reading (or re-reading) all Jane Austen's novels in order of
publication (which is how I've dealt with them in the
critical introductions) and back to back. I know, because I
recently did it, and it was an unusual privilege. Throw in
some time with the *Letters to Cassandra*, and as any Janeite
will tell you, you start to feel Miss Austen's presence to an
uncanny degree, accompanied by a strong desire for her
still to be alive, so that you might meet her, quiz her, try to
understand her. This may well be untrue of almost any
other writer of fiction you can name; but it's certainly true
for her.

So, to begin: How *did* she do it?

I

JANE AUSTEN – THE LIFE

A biography of Jane Austen is, in many ways, straightforward enough – her life neatly divides into two unequal parts. The first thirty-six years saw her living a relatively sequestered existence, unknown outside her circle of friends and family, a correct, impecunious, Hampshire spinster with a sharp turn of phrase. The remaining six years of her life were those in which she became a published novelist, acquired a modest reputation, and left behind the works that would eventually confirm her position as one of the most durable and important writers in the English language.

More good news, from the biographer's point of view, is that she was an indefatigable and candid letter-writer. Her surviving correspondence not only yields many insights into the world in which she lived, but gratifyingly speaks with the same voice, the same wit and acuity as do her novels.

The bad news is that Cassandra Austen, her sister, confidante and most dependable correspondent, destroyed enormous numbers of Jane's letters after her death in 1817. Other letters were lost or destroyed by other family members and friends as her reputation began to grow in the mid-nineteenth century. Her nephew and first biographer, James Edward Austen-Leigh, was careful to suppress some of her earlier material. Why? The best guess seems to be that as Jane's fame grew, and as the differences between Regency and Victorian sensibilities became more pointed, so it became increasingly important to preserve her reputation – and that of her family – from any perceptible lapses of taste which might have been found in her unpublished writings.

As a result, any view of Miss Austen's life tends towards the lopsided. Where letters do exist, they reveal useful information and valuable material for conjecture. Where they don't, there's usually a gap, unfilled by other sources. Who would have been keeping an account, after all? No one knew how big the Austen industry would get. Faced with a wealth of material, and an equally impressive wealth of gaps, Jane Austen's biographers are frequently reduced to padding out the story of her life with tales of her illustrious seafaring brothers, or her racy Anglo-French cousin.

This much we do know: Jane Austen was born on 16 December 1775, at Steventon, in Hampshire. Her father, the Revd George Austen, was the Oxford-educated rector of Steventon, with an additional responsibility for the nearby parish of Deane. Civilized, tolerant and from every account an extremely likeable human being, his main struggle in life was with money: he was always poor, and frequently in debt.

His wife, Cassandra Leigh, came from a family with connections to both land and titles, and found it something of a struggle to adapt to George's level of genteel penury. Nevertheless, she was energetic and sharp-witted. She was also a busy mother, bearing eight children between the years 1765 and 1779 before deciding that enough was enough, and that she would spend the rest of her life as something of a valetudinarian.

James, the first son, became a clergyman, and would eventually inherit his father's position at Steventon. George, the second son, was born handicapped and spent his life in care, living away from the rest of the family. Edward Austen was – in the manner of the times – given away at around the age of fifteen for adoption by wealthy, childless, relatives at Godmersham, in Kent. Henry Austen drifted entertainingly from the military, to banking (where he later went bust), to – at last – the Church. Cassandra Austen was to live a life in parallel with her sister's – never marrying, but being immortalized as the recipient of Jane's letters. Frank Austen had a terrific career in the Royal Navy, ending his days as Sir Francis Austen, Admiral of the Fleet. Jane, the penultimate child, was succeeded by Charles Austen, who enjoyed a Naval career almost as glittering as that of his brother Frank: he too, became an Admiral.

To add to this mix of progeny (and increase his small

income) the Revd George Austen took in pupils, among them young Lord Lymington, Lord Portsmouth's son. The rectory at Steventon was thus kept in a state of bustling turbulence, even as the older Austens left their family home. The cellar flooded regularly, the kitchen garden needed constant attention, there were boys everywhere, the servants – a minimal establishment – had to be overseen, the physical condition of the main house (despite extensive repairs) was poor and the rectory smallholding, with its cows, pigs, chickens and ducks, didn't bring in much money. This was what Jane Austen knew until she was six years old – at which point she and Cassandra were sent to boarding school in Oxford.

This move, too, was in the manner of the times. The sisters were enrolled at an establishment run by Mrs Cawley, widow of a former Principal of Brasenose College, who hauled them round the colleges, before decamping with them to Southampton. There, both Jane and Cassandra caught the 'putrid fever' – probably typhus – and nearly died. In a panic, their mother extricated them while Mr Austen redirected them to the Abbey School at Reading. There, a 'Mrs Latournelle' – actually Miss Sarah Hackett – gave them a basic education.

By 1786 Jane was back at home, having improved her reading, practised her sewing (she was particularly adept at satin stitch) and gained some knowledge of French. She also learned the piano – an instrument that became central to her conception of civilized life. She acquired a music teacher, George Chard, and would later write, 'I am glad to hear so good an account of Mr Charde, and only fear that my long absence may occasion his relapse. I practise every day as much as I can – I wish it were more for his sake.' She read Samuel Johnson and Samuel Richardson (who would later come to influence some of her writing). She talked with her brothers as they came and went, and met her glamorous cousin, Eliza, Comtesse de Feuillide, who was born a Hancock but married into the French aristocracy.

At this age, she was still something of a work-in-progress. When her sharp-tongued cousin, Philadelphia Walter, came to dine, the latter wrote of the Austen sisters, 'The youngest' – Jane – 'is very like her brother Henry, not at all pretty and very prim, unlike a girl of twelve.' When the Austens returned the visit, she went on, 'They spent the day with us, and the more I see of Cassandra the more I admire – Jane is whimsical and affected.'

But at least Jane had begun to write.

Between 1787 and 1793, she pecked away at those pieces now generically referred to as the *Juvenilia*. Twenty-nine instances of *Juvenilia* still exist, copies written out in three notebooks that were given to her by her father. They bear titles such as *Jack & Alice*, *Love and Freindship* (a not untypical misspelling), *The History of England*, *Lesley Castle* and *The Adventures of Mr. Harley*. They vary wildly in quality. And they do not read like Jane Austen.

Given that Fielding and Richardson would have been Miss Austen's models, it makes sense that there is vastly more bad behaviour (drunkenness, hysteria, poisoning, insolence towards a parent) in the *Juvenilia* than in any of her mature works, not to mention a good deal more callousness. A case in point: 'My sister came running to me in the store-room,' explains a character in *Lesley Castle*, with her face as White as a Whipt syllabub, and told me that Hervey had been thrown from his Horse, had fractured his Scull and was pronounced by his surgeon to be in the most emminent Danger. "Good God! (said I) you dont say so? Why what in the name of Heaven will become of all the Victuals! We shall never be able to eat it while it is good. However, we'll call in the Surgeon to help us. I shall be able to manage the Sir-loin myself, my Mother will eat the soup, and You and the Doctor must finish the rest."

Love and Freindship was slightly less robust in tone, and Jane thought highly enough of the finished work to dedicate it to Eliza de Feuillide, having first stuffed it with highly charged epistolary Richardsonian moments. As Lindsay, 'The son of an English Baronet', recounts:

'"Never let it be said that I obliged my Father."
    We all admired the noble Manliness of his reply. He continued.
    "Sir Edward was surprised; he had perhaps little expected to meet with so spirited an opposition to his will." Where, Edward in the name of wonder (said he) did you pick up this unmeaning gibberish? You have been studying Novels I suspect." I scorned to answer: it would have been beneath my dignity.'

And, several pages later: 'To compleat such unparalelled Barbarity we were informed that an Execution in the House would shortly take place. Ah! what could we do but what we did! We sighed and fainted on the sofa.'
    And several pages after that: '"Base Miscreant! (cried I) how canst thou thus undauntedly endeavour to sully the

spotless reputation of such bright Excellence? Why dost thou not suspect MY innocence as soon?"'

And so on. This is fine teenage stuff, vulgar in the best way, often very funny, and would, when read aloud to the Austen family (which it undoubtedly was) have had its audience in stitches. Clearly, young Jane was sharp, had a talent for writing and wanted to show off this talent to those – like Eliza – who meant something to her.

Indeed, she began yet another epistolary novel, later called *Lady Susan*, which was inspired by her cousin Eliza's dynamic love life – much of which now involved Jane's own brother, Henry. *Lady Susan* is a startlingly energetic compendium of ruses, foiled love affairs, stagy outpourings, but with a visibly darker tone than the earlier parodies. 'I had intended to write to Reginald myself as soon as my eyes would let me,' says the scheming Lady de Courcy fretfully, 'to point out, as well as I could, the danger of an intimate acquaintance, with so artful a woman as Lady Susan.' But to no avail. 'That tormenting creature, Reginald, is here,' Lady Susan announces, audibly rubbing her hands. 'Much as I wish him away, however, I cannot help being pleased with such a proof of attachment. He is devoted to me, heart and soul.' She has worse in store for him as the book progresses. 'Humbled as he now is, I cannot forgive him such an instance of pride, and am doubtful whether I ought not to punish him by dismissing him at once after this reconciliation, or by marrying and teazing him for ever.' Elsewhere, the melodrama seethes away: 'I am in agonies . . . a very weak young man . . . I could have poisoned him – diabolical scheme . . . abominable trick . . .' Headlong and tempestuous, the plot is only brought to halt with a *de facto* admission of defeat by the author: 'This correspondence, by a meeting between some of the parties, and a separation between the others, could not, to the great detriment of the Post Office revenue, be continued any longer.' The story ends with a comic deflation. Jane had explored a more destructive, perverse, kind of psychology, and now, having made her experiment, she was done with it. But what happened next?

What happened next was probably the now-lost *Elinor and Marianne*, which, according to Cassandra, Jane began at some time during her late teens, perhaps in 1795. This would eventually become *Sense and Sensibility*, but not before she had tired altogether of the limitations of the epistolary form and reworked it into something that more closely resembled her first published novel, before losing interest in that too. In 1796 she began a new (and equally vanished) story, *First Impressions*. This, in turn, would become *Pride and Prejudice*, but only many years later and after much reconstruction.

Something had changed. Parodies and burlesques; storm-tossed aristocrats and heaving plotlines: these were being dropped in favour of a quieter, more rational approach, one a good deal closer to home. Jane had decided to engage with the world around her, and with her own feelings towards it.

The world, at any rate, was engaging with the Austen sisters. Cassandra had fallen in love with Tom Fowle, an impecunious young cleric, and friend of the family. This was no flirtation: the two were affianced before Fowle's relative, Lord Craven, made him an intriguing job offer. He would take the young man off to the West Indies as his regimental chaplain. To the young lovers, it must have seemed like a good idea. If all went well, Tom would return a few years later, sufficiently well set up to be able to marry Cassandra.

Jane, too, was exploring the possibilities of romance. She was now of an age to attend the many balls (ranging from relatively impromptu get-togethers, to larger, more formal events) which punctuated country social life. It was enough to have four couples and a competent pianist in your front rooms for a dance to take place. The monthly Assembly Balls at Basingstoke may not sound much, but would have been public, reasonably well-attended and eminently appealing, in their constrained, heavily chaperoned way. An old, and non-too-reliable, family acquaintance remembered the young, social, ball-going Jane of the 1790s as 'The prettiest, silliest, most affected, husband-hunting butterfly.'

This raises the question of what Jane actually looked like. The only contemporary likeness in existence – unless we include the disputed picture of Jane, unearthed in 2011 – is the one drawn by Cassandra, somewhat later in life, which shows her with tired eyes, a pursed mouth and a beaky nose. Far better portraits exist of the Austen men – the Revd George, brothers Frank, Charles and Henry – all of which suggest a remarkably good-looking family, with penetrating gazes and lordly noses, features which sit well with them, but which would look less good on a young woman. What consensus there is suggests that Jane was not strikingly good-looking, but a long way from plain: she had light brown eyes, curling brown hair, full, pink, cheeks. She was slim, poised in her movements – and she loved to dance.

And it's clear that (allowing for the proprieties of the time) she took the opportunity to flirt when it presented itself. But with whom? The surviving letters now start to provide evidence, although they don't always make her preferences in men very clear. She writes to Cassandra at the start of 1796, 'I danced twice with Warren last night, and once with Mr Charles Watkins, and, to my inexpressible astonishment, I entirely escaped John Lyford. I was forced to fight hard for it, however.' She later writes, 'We had a visit yesterday morning from Mr Benjamin Portal, whose eyes are as handsome as ever.' Moreover, she refers, archly, to 'All my other admirers,' and 'The kiss which C. Powlett wanted to give me.' And she had a playful crush on Edward Taylor, later MP for Canterbury – alluded to in the throwaway line, 'We went by Bifrons, & I contemplated with a melancholy pleasure, the abode of Him, on whom I once fondly doated.'

There is, though, a clear favourite, and his name is Tom Lefroy. The nephew of Mrs Anne Lefroy, a close family friend, Tom was over from Ireland at the very end of 1795. Bookish and moneyless, he had come to study law in England; eventually he became Ireland's Lord Chief Justice, but at the time his material prospects were vanishingly slender. Was there a *tendresse* between him and the twenty-year-old Jane? Very likely. Years later he would describe his own feelings for Jane as 'A boy's love'; enough of an endorsement. Is there a way of calibrating Jane's emotional state? The best bet seems to be to consider the importance that Tom Lefroy briefly assumes in her letters.

The first letter in any anthology of Jane Austen's correspondence will almost invariably be one dated 9 January

1796 – to Cassandra, on the occasion of her twenty-third birthday. This begins: 'In the first place I hope you will live twenty-three years longer. Mr Tom Lefroy's birthday was yesterday, so that you are very near of an age.' Her dear sister and her new best friend share that opening paragraph, equally prominent in her affections.

She then comes over all coquettish, announcing that 'I am almost afraid to tell you how my Irish friend' – Tom Lefroy again – 'and I behaved. Imagine to yourself everything most profligate and shocking in the way of dancing and sitting down together.' Later on, she assures Cassandra that 'He is a very gentlemanlike, good-looking, pleasant young man, I assure you ... he is so excessively laughed at about me at Ashe, that he is ashamed of coming to Steventon, and ran away when we called on Mrs Lefroy a few days ago.' She then goes on to write about other things before returning to the subject of the young Mr Lefroy, noting his '*One* fault, which time will, I trust, entirely remove – it is that his morning coat is a great deal too light. He is a very great admirer of Tom Jones' – the fictitious hero who dressed in a light, rather than fashionably dark, coat – 'and therefore wears the same coloured clothes.'

Several days later, she writes about him again – 'I mean to confine myself in future to Mr Tom Lefroy, for whom I do not care sixpence' – and *again*, a day after that: 'The day is come on which I am to flirt my last with Tom Lefroy, and when you receive this it will be over. My tears flow as I write at the melancholy idea.' Given the informal, fragmented nature of many of her letters, skipping from topic to topic, occasionally leaving thoughts and sentences unfinished, it's striking how much coherent space she devotes to Lefroy. She gives the impression, all in all, of not being able to drop the subject; of being unable to stop thinking about him.

Does this necessarily indicate a sentimental attachment? One might argue that Jane didn't particularly care for Tom and was only writing in this teasing way to entertain Cassandra. An equally plausible explanation is that she did care, but, unnerved by her own feelings, attempted to draw their sting by mocking them. Jane may not have known what she felt. But the sheer weight of repetition in her letters to her sister tells its own story.

At last Tom left – very possibly urged on by his family, who were keen for him not to marry the penniless daughter of an impoverished clergyman. Nor did he return. In fact he only reappears in the letters a couple of years later, unnamed and unnamable, as an emblem of regret in one of Jane's encounters with Mrs Lefroy. 'Of her nephew,' Jane wrote,

> she said nothing at all, and of her friend very little. She did not once mention the name of the former to *me*, and I was too proud to make any enquiries; but on my father's afterwards asking where he was, I learnt that he was gone back to London in his way to Ireland, where he is called to the bar and means to practise.

There would be other, less convincing, suitors in Jane's future. She would not be completely ignored. But there is poignancy in the way she is compelled to linger over the awkwardness of mentioning Lefroy's name, and the details of his new life in Ireland. Convention paints Jane Austen as a maidenly retiree, unable fully to engage in the passions that animate her characters – a starchy observer; a spinster. But it's more likely that she loved and suffered and had regrets, much like anyone else. Her novels are not built on hearsay.

By the spring of 1797, though, Cassandra's love life had collapsed in ruins. Her fiancé, Tom Fowle, had died of yellow fever in the West Indies. Lord Craven declared, unhelpfully, that if he had known of the engagement, he would never have taken Tom to such a dangerous place. Cassandra went into a stoical mourning.

No letters exist for the period 1796 through to early 1798. During this time, the chances for Jane and Cassandra to escape their condition seem to disappear. By the time the letters do resume, it's as if the two women have become set in the roles they would occupy for the rest of their lives. Cassandra has gone from being a woman in love – as well as 'The finest comic writer of the present age', as Jane buoyantly calls her at the start of a letter from 1796 – to the mute, unmarriageable mirror of Jane's brilliance.

Jane, meanwhile, has settled for life as a spinster on a pinched allowance of £20 a year, fussing ironically over her appearance ('Next week [I] shall begin operations on my hat, on which you know my principal hopes of happiness depend'), looking after the comfortably invalid Mrs Austen ('I had the dignity of dropping out my mother's laudanum last night') and seeing to the efficient running of the house at Steventon ('I carry about the keys of the wine and closet, and twice since I began this letter have had orders to give in the kitchen'). Men still appear from time to time, including an enormous, tedious theologian called Samuel Blackall ('There seems no likelihood of his coming into Hampshire this Christmas,' Jane recorded, 'and it is therefore most probable that our indifference will soon be mutual, unless his regard, which appeared to spring from knowing nothing of me at first, is best supported by never seeing me'). Balls and social encounters come and go. But as the two women gradually age (both in their twenties, that crucial decade for marriage) so the sense of opportunity, of fun, gradually dwindles.

George Austen made an effort to help by offering *First Impressions* to Cadell, a London publisher, on behalf of his daughter. He sent no copy of the text, instead describing the work as 'A manuscript novel, comprising 3 volumes'. Cadell refused by return of post. This failure did at least remind Jane of what she wanted to do, in between tending to her mother and perfecting her sewing technique ('I am proud to say that I am the neatest worker of the party'), and in November 1797, she began *Sense and Sensibility* – her new take on *Elinor and Marianne*. The following year, she made a start on *Northanger Abbey*.

Her world was thus set for a while. In the autumn of 1798, Jane, Cassandra, the Revd and Mrs Austen made the journey from Steventon (in Hampshire) to Godmersham (in Kent), where Edward Austen Knight had succeeded to the mid-eighteenth century big house, with its handsome frontage and its landscaped grounds. Cassandra then stayed on at Godmersham, while the others returned home. On the way back, Jane's writing and dressing boxes were almost lost, along with her 'worldly wealth' of £7. A trunk nearly fell off the coach a couple of days later. They got back to Steventon, where laudanum made Mrs Austen 'sleep a good deal', and Jane and her father sat down and dined by themselves. 'How strange!' Jane noted, surprised by the quietness of the family home, now without sons, paying pupils, or Cassandra.

The narrowness of her life continued. 'I am very fond of experimental housekeeping,' she wrote to her absent sister, 'such as having an ox-cheek now and then; I shall have one next week, and I mean to have some little dumplings put into it, that I may fancy myself at Godmersham.' A week later, she complained that 'The ball on Thursday was a very small one indeed, hardly so large as an Oxford smack. There were but seven couples, and only twenty-seven people in the room.' Three weeks after that she notes: 'We dine now at half after Three' – unfashionably early – '& have done dinner I suppose before you begin – We drink tea at half after six. – I am afraid you will despise us. – My father reads Cowper to us in the evening, to which I listen when I can.'

William Cowper sounds about right: his retiring, domestic, faintly melancholy verse ('The morning finds the self-sequestered man/Fresh for his task, intend what task he may') and his quietly Evangelical religious leanings ('God moves in a mysterious way/His wonders to perform') would have sat well in the scene of pallid gentility which Jane conjures up in her writings. A gentility is enlivened, in fact, only by Mrs Austen's condition: 'Her Bowels are still not entirely settled, & she sometimes complains of an Asthma, a Dropsy, Water in her Chest & a Liver Disorder.'

The New Year came and went, and the sadness becomes more perceptible. Jane's eyes were giving her trouble ('The more I write, the better my eye gets') and she went to a ball where

> I do not think I was very much in request. People were rather apt not to ask me till they could not help it ... There was one gentleman, an officer of the Cheshire, a very good-looking young man, who, I was told, wanted very much to be introduced to me; but as he did not want it quite enough to take much trouble in effecting it, we never could bring it about.

Her distemper even vented itself against Cassandra. 'I do not wonder at your wanting to read "First Impressions" again,' she wrote, tetchily, 'so seldom as you have gone through it, and that so long ago.'

Only the business of creating *Susan*, the novel that eventually became *Northanger Abbey*, must have given Jane much satisfaction. Here at least, she was making tangible progress towards a writing style. Epistolary forms and overwrought characters were giving way to what one now recognizes as the Austen voice. The *Northanger Abbey* that finally appeared, many years after she originally wrote *Susan*, depicts characters that have some kind of authenticity about them; and it tells their stories in an early version of the free indirect style of which she showed such mastery later on.

It also has another innovation: a proper sense of place – and that place is Bath. Edward Austen Knight and his wife,

Elizabeth, had determined to visit Bath in order to find relief for Edward's gout. They decamped from Godmersham, while Cassandra returned to Steventon, before taking Jane and Mrs Austen with them, in the spring of 1799. They were all installed at 13 Queen Square, from where Jane wrote to Cassandra that, 'We are exceedingly pleased with the house'. But her feelings towards the rest of Bath were mixed.

She had been to Bath before, at the end of 1797, with her mother and Cassandra. She said of her arrival in 1799, 'It has rained almost all the way, and our first view of Bath has been just as gloomy as it was last November twelvemonth.' Never a town person ('Here I am once more in this scene of dissipation and vice, and I begin already to find my morals corrupted,' she once wrote of London), her spirits didn't respond any better to this novelty city. Laid out by the John Woods, father and son, some forty years earlier, Bath would now have been at an uneasy point of decline. By the end of the eighteenth century, Bath had lost its pre-eminent fashionability to Brighton and Cheltenham. Beau Nash, the great custodian of Bath society, was long dead; and it found itself simultaneously too recently established to boast the charms of age, too *vieux jeu* to attract the smart set, too insistent on form and appearance to be at all comfortable. Shopping, taking the waters, receiving consultations from mildly fraudulent doctors, attending dances and musical entertainments: that was what one could expect from Bath. In its favour, it was at least thought tame enough to appeal to modest provincials like the Austens.

Jane's well-heeled uncle, James Leigh Perrot, and her

aunt, Jane Leigh Perrot, were also there. Uncle James's chronic gout, like brother Edward's, was the excuse. James was amiable and tolerant enough, but Aunt Perrot, although not without redeeming qualities – she could be financially generous – was overbearing, critical and self-righteous. As a consequence of all this – the ennui, the stuffiness, the limited company – Jane's appreciation of the city struggled to rise above the grudging: 'At present I have no great notion of staying here above a month'; 'I spent friday evening with the Mapletons, & was obliged to submit to being pleased in spite of my inclination'; 'The concert will have more than it's usual charm with me, as the gardens are large enough for me to get pretty well beyond the reach of its sound'; 'I feel tolerably secure of our getting away next week'; 'We have not been to any public place lately'; 'The Play on Saturday is *I hope* to conclude our Gaieties here'.

But it did give her something to write about. No one would call *Northanger Abbey* an unqualified success, not least because of its failure to knit the two narrative locations – Bath and Northanger Abbey – satisfactorily together. But at least when Jane writes at the start of Chapter 3, 'Every morning now brought its regular duties; – shops were to be visited; some new part of the town to be looked at; and the Pump-room to be attended, where they paraded up and down for an hour, looking at every body and speaking to no one,' Bath makes sense as a setting for the action. It generates narrative opportunities. It seems realized.

Jane returned to Steventon, finished *Susan* and took up her usual round. There were more balls of the kind she was comfortable with – not the bleak parade in the Upper

Rooms at Bath. The only problem was a shortage of male dancing partners. Britain's protracted war with France had taken many young men into the Navy, the regular Army and the Militia. Jane noted the consequences of this at one ball, where 'I danced nine dances out of ten, five with Stephen Terry, T. Chute & James Digweed & four with Catherine. There was commonly a couple of Ladies standing up together, but not often any so amiable as ourselves.'

The Revd George Austen was less sanguine, on account of money worries ('The farm cleared £300 last year'), and the entire family was thrown into mild panic by a great storm one day in November 1800. At the sound of crashes from outside, Jane hurried to the window 'Just in time to see the last of our two highly valued Elms descend into the Sweep!!!!!' There was worse:

> One large Elm out of two on the left hand side, as you enter what I call the Elm walk, was likewise blown down, the Maypole bearing the weathercock was broke in two, and what I regret more than all the rest, is that all the three Elms which grew in Hall's meadow & gave such ornament to it, are gone.

Jane recovered from this upset by staying with her old and dear friend Martha Lloyd at Ibthorpe, not far away. 'Martha looks very well, & wants me to find out that she grows fat; but I cannot carry my complaisance farther than to believe whatever she asserts on the subject,' she wrote with amused tartness.

* * *

Everything had settled in its semi-dependable way, in other words, until Jane got back from Martha Lloyd's. At this point she discovered that George Austen had decided to quit Steventon and move his nuclear family – Jane and Mrs Austen – back to Bath, of all places. Son James would take over the house and the living at Steventon. Twenty-five years of continuity were about to be broken up. The story goes that Jane was so appalled at the news, she fainted.

The Revd Austen's motives were understandable. He was nearly seventy; the Steventon house was far too large and expensive to keep up, especially for the reduced Austen household, where at least one daughter was always away, visiting. His health was also not outstandingly good, and the waters at Bath might help. Aunt Perrot maintained that the family had to move in order to separate Jane from the attentions of one of the Digweed sons, but it's also – just – possible that the Austen parents thought that Jane and Cassandra might increase their chances of meeting a suitable husband in the *va et vient* of the town.

Jane's letters from this time were stoical. There was much appraisal of possible houses in Bath; similar discussion of furnishings and possessions at Steventon; urgings from Jane for Cassandra (back, once more, at Godmersham) to be sure to join her in Bath as soon as possible; and occasional, intelligible, notes of regret.

'I get more & more reconciled to the idea of our removal,' she wrote in early January 1801. 'We have lived long enough in this Neighbourhood, the Basingstoke Balls are certainly on the decline, there is something interesting in the bustle of going away, & the prospect of spending future summers by the Sea or in Wales is very delightful.'

But a couple of lines later, she added, 'It must not be generally known however that I am not sacrificing a great deal in quitting the Country.' Meanwhile, Cassandra had no desire immediately to join Jane and Mrs Austen in Bath (George Austen would arrive in his own time), so Jane waved her away with a brittle 'Do as you like; I have overcome my desire of your going to Bath with my mother and me.'

The paintings that hung at Steventon were divided up among the family. George Austen put hundreds of his precious books up for sale, along with his chest of drawers and study table. Jane's piano was sold. It was decided that Mr and Mrs Austen would have to take their bed down to Bath with them, as it was the only thing they could comfortably sleep on. Jane's clothes and small possessions were packed up into the usual couple of trunks.

And then, in May, Jane was reacquainted with the city. Her 'First view of Bath in fine weather,' grimly enough, 'does not answer my expectations.' She wished, morosely, for rain to improve the scene. 'The sun was got behind everything, and the appearance of the place from the top of Kingsdown was all vapour, shadow, smoke, and confusion.' After that, it was all a question of finding the right place to live, doing the best one could with the pervasive dampness of the accommodation, hob-nobbing with the elderly Leigh Perrots, wondering at the thinness of society.

A week into her enforced stay, Jane was grumbling to Cassandra about the entertainment after tea at the Assembly Rooms. 'There was only one dance, danced by four couple. – Think of four couple, surrounded by about an hundred people, dancing in the upper Rooms at Bath!'

After tea, fortunately enough, 'the breaking up of private parties sent some scores more to the Ball, & tho' it was shockingly & inhumanly thin for this place, there were people enough I suppose to have made five or six very pretty Basingstoke assemblies.' The next day, she wrote about 'Another stupid party last night; perhaps if larger they might be less intolerable, but here there were only just enough to make one card table, with six people to look on, & talk nonsense to each other.' And then, some days after that, 'We are to have a tiny party here tonight; I hate tiny parties – they force one into constant exertion.' The company lacked style. Miss Twisleton (a relative) was 'Highly rouged, & looked rather quietly and contentedly silly than anything else'. A Miss Langley was 'Like any other short girl with a broad nose & wide mouth, fashionable dress, & exposed bosom'; while Admiral Stanhope was 'A gentlemanlike Man, but his legs are too short, & his tail too long.' Another party 'Was not quite so stupid as the two preceding parties here.' The futility and disappointment of it all rises from the page.

It was also proving hard to find somewhere to live – available properties turned out to be plagued by 'Discontented families & putrid fevers', and only useful for providing some cranky entertainment for her and Cassandra. 'When you arrive,' she wrote to her sister, 'we will at least have the pleasure of examining some of these putrifying Houses again; – they are so very desirable in size & situation, that there is some satisfaction in spending ten minutes within them.' Some properties in New King Street interested her mother, 'But their size has now satisfied her; – they were smaller than I expected to find them. One in particular out of the two, was quite monstrously little; – the best of the sitting-rooms not so large as the little parlour at Steventon, and the second room in every floor about capacious enough to admit a very small bed.' A prospective landlord was 'Willing to raise the kitchen floor' in order to keep the dampness at bay: 'But all this I fear is fruitless – tho' the water may be kept out of sight, it cannot be sent away, nor the ill effects of its nearness be excluded.'

About the only good news, in fact, was that Mrs Austen was 'Very well,' having been 'quite free from feverish or bilious complaints since her arrival here.' There was that, and a ride to the top of Kingsdown in a 'Very bewitching Phaeton & four' carriage with a well-known old charmer, Mr Evelyn – who was allegedly in the middle of an extramarital affair with the highly rouged Miss Twisleton. Clearly, the element of naughtiness was no problem: if anything, it added to Jane's sense of occasion, of daring to be different to the dullards in town.

And then the letters stop. The last surviving letter of 1801 (to Cassandra) ends, 'Unless anything particular occurs I shall not write again.' The next is dated 1804. Three opaque years go by.

What is clear – according to the surviving relatives – is that Jane, Cassandra and their parents spent part of the summer in Sidmouth, Devon, where Jane had a brief liaison with a tall, personable, clergyman, with whom she walked on the promenade. He was so personable, in fact, that he asked – and was given – permission to join the Austens later in the year. And then he died. The similarity between Jane's circumstances and Cassandra's at the death of her fiancé

Tom Fowle, is almost too novelish, too artfully symmetrical. But that is what seems to have happened. According to Louisa Lefroy, Jane's great-niece, the unknown cleric was 'One of the most charming persons' Cassandra had ever known. According to Louisa's sister *Fanny* Lefroy, the shared heartbreak 'Endeared the two sisters to each other and made other sympathy unnecessary to each.' The word *love* was retroactively bandied around; Jane's thoughts on the matter are, naturally, lost.

So in 1801 the Austens returned to Bath, to 4 Sydney Place, where they had finally found somewhere bearable to live. A year passed. The routine re-established itself. Jane and Cassandra, having consoled one another, went, in November 1802, to stay with James and Mary Austen, back at Steventon. From there, they paid a call on the Biggs at Manydown – family friends who lived in great squirarchal comfort near Basingstoke, in Hampshire, under the paternalistic gaze of Manydown's owner, Lovelace Bigg Wither. Here there was *another* failed romance, which ended this time not by death or departure, but by Jane's own choice.

It seems that Lovelace's son, young Harris Bigg Wither, aged twenty-one, conceived a fondness for Jane, who was very nearly twenty-seven. She was in the house for all of a week before he proposed marriage to her. What chance did he have of acceptance? The age gap was not in itself a terrible obstacle – Jane's brother Henry had married the widowed Eliza de Feuillide, ten years his senior, with some success – but Harris Bigg Wither's personality was.

History has not been especially kind to Harris Bigg Wither. Any consequence he enjoys is due entirely to his fleeting relationship with Jane Austen, and to resulting efforts to put some sort of face to his name. Apparently, he was big, maladroit, uncouth and had a stutter. At a loss in polite company, and hindered by his speech impediment, he tended not to say much; but what he did say was short on charm. According to one relative, Harris addressed a gathering of friends with the words: 'In your individual capacity you are all very good fellows, but in your corporate capacity you are very disagreeable,' before sitting down and concentrating on the glass of bad punch that had occasioned his remarks.

What did he see in Jane? More to the point, what did she see in him? Because not only did he propose to her – she accepted him. She then endured a sleepless night, turning the prospect of marriage to Harris Bigg Wither over in her mind, met with him in the morning, broke the engagement off and demanded an immediate return to Steventon.

Twenty-seven was a trying age to be. Jane would have been pretty much at the limit of what was considered a proper marriageable age – at least for the first round. She must have brooded on the respectability and relative safety that would have come with marriage to Harris Bigg Wither and the world of material comfort that would have been hers. She would equally have dwelt on the counter-prospect of years of impoverished spinsterhood, which would be all that was left if she didn't marry him. She might even have tried to persuade herself that Harris Bigg Wither's asininity was an asset – making him easy to out-think, and therefore more tractable as a husband.

But she bravely spurned him, hurried back to Steventon in the Bigg Withers' carriage, and then – according to her niece, Caroline Austen – obliged brother James to take both her and Cassandra all the way back to Bath, to put as much distance between herself and Manydown as possible.

So the year ended on a note of recapitulation, with the Austens temporarily housed in Bath, Jane and Cassandra condemned to spinsterhood, Mrs Austen complacently noting that the two sisters were effectively 'Wedded to each other'. There was no prospect of anything changing – unless it involved Jane's stalled career as a novelist.

In recognition of this, Jane's father stirred himself again to offer one of her books to a publisher. This time the work was *Northanger Abbey* (or *Susan*, as it was then being called). Things seemed to turn out rather better than they had for *First Impressions*, and the manuscript was accepted by Messrs Crosby & Cox, who paid £10 for the rights: Jane's first professional sale. Ten pounds wasn't a huge amount (successful published authors such as Fanny Burney could command twenty times as much, with ease) and Crosby & Cox refused to say when they would actually publish the work. Indeed, they were under no obligation to do anything at all with it, and so the manuscript sat in their London offices gathering dust, awaiting a moment of publication which never came.

It was still a sale, though, and enough to re-awaken some of Jane's energies. Between 1803–1805 she started work on the novel fragment known as *The Watsons*.

In this, evidently, she was using her writing to address the concerns of real life. The family at the centre of the story is genteel but indigent, with two sisters who urgently need to be married off for fear that they will 'Grow old and be poor and be laughed at.' Moreover, there is a brother who has done well at the Law, and whose success points up the relative hopelessness of the sisters. Among the Johnsonian aphorisms – 'When an old Lady plays the fool, it is not in the course of nature that she should suffer from it many years' – there are echoes of Jane's letters – 'She danced twice with Captain Hunter, and I think shews him in general as much Encouragement as is consistent with her disposition, and the circumstances she is placed in.' There is even a glimpse of the Austens' social scene, in the way 'The cold and empty appearance of the Room and the demure air of the small cluster of Females at one end of it began soon to give way; the inspiriting sound of other Carriages was heard, and continual accessions of portly Chaperons, and strings of smartly-dressed girls were received, with now and then a fresh gentleman straggler.' And there are a handful of undependable suitors. What exists of *The Watsons*, in other words, is credible enough; it reads a bit like Jane Austen. The temptation is to see it in full light of retrospection, a necessary step on Jane's path to becoming the celebrated author – a goal some way in the distance, but increasingly within reach.

In fact, Jane, in her thirtieth year, was starting to resemble one of her own *Watsons* characters. Her brothers were all (apart from the invalid George) married and making their ways in the world, while she and Cassandra were completely dependent on their surviving parents, friends and relations to accommodate them and give them financial subventions. All Jane had were her Christian piety and her humorous, critical, intelligence to make sense of the world. These seemed enough, as she wrote in the autumn of 1804 from Lyme Regis: 'I continue quite well; in proof of which I have bathed again this morning. It was absolutely necessary that I should have the little fever and indisposition which I had; it has been all the fashion this week in Lyme.' She was feeling brighter; the tone of her letters was such that Cassandra felt she could leave them to posterity.

And then, like Emma and Elizabeth Watson, they were deprived of a parent. In January 1805, decent, thoughtful, George Austen died.

There was a convulsion in the Austen family, with the brothers determining what sums of money they needed to contribute in order to keep their mother and sisters afloat. Both Frank and James, the least well provided for, were handsome in their offers. After some shuffling of resources, about £450 a year was found for the three women: a nicely judged stipend, at a time when the war with the French was driving prices up. Jane's annual outgoings would include £14 for clothing and £6 for presents. Having already moved from Sydney Place to Green Park Buildings, Jane, Cassandra and Mrs Austen decamped to Gay Street with one maid, in order to save money. Tea and sugar were enjoyed sparingly: 'We cannot be supposed to be very rich.'

These were the two sharp new realities in Jane's life: her father, and all his consolations, was gone; and she was now obliged to her siblings for almost every material thing. Money, never exactly a source of contented hilarity, became positively oppressive. When Jane went to visit her brother Edward and his wife Elizabeth at smart Godmersham, she was sadly grateful for being charged a reduced fee by the visiting hairdresser: 'Towards me he was considerate, as I had hoped for . . . charging me only 2/6d for cutting my hair ... He certainly respects either our youth or our poverty.' At the same time, the cost of tipping the maid, Sackree, burdened her – 'As I find on looking into my affairs, that instead of being very rich I am likely to be very poor, I cannot afford more than ten shillings for Sackree'. She was burdened, in fact, by an inescapable sense of being disadvantaged. 'It is well,' she wrote to Cassandra, 'to prepare you for the sight of a Sister sunk in poverty, that it may not overcome your Spirits.' A tiresome acquaintance, Mrs Stent, who had previously been jeered at in the letters – 'Mrs Stent gives us quite as much of her company as we wish for, & rather more than she used to' – re-emerged in a sadder, more reflective light: 'Perhaps in time we may come to be Mrs Stents ourselves, unequal to anything & unwelcome to everybody.' There was not much to look forward to.

In the end, the best thing that could happen, happened. The Austens left Bath. It was now the summer of 1806, and the process that would eventually take Jane to Chawton in Hampshire had begun. Chawton would be her final home, and the place that would allow her, one way or another, to become a writer. Later, she would observe, 'It will be two years tomorrow since we left Bath for Clifton, with what happy feelings of Escape!' In the meantime, there was a good deal of movement around England to be accomplished, including a visit to country mansion Stoneleigh Abbey in Warwickshire, where relatives kept Jane in some style; before Jane, Cassandra and Mrs Austen descended on the relatively crowded Southampton home of Naval brother Frank.

Frank was currently between ships, having just missed the action at the Battle of Trafalgar (1805), and was short of money. But the family managed to cram themselves in somehow, and the next year saw them move into a more spacious residence in Castle Square, not far from the waterfront. 'We hear,' Jane wrote, 'that we are envied our House by many people, & that the Garden is the best in the Town.' Here there was a good deal of sewing, and more travelling. Significantly, the three female Austens went to visit Edward Austen Knight at Chawton House, part of his Hampshire estate. They also saw James Austen at Steventon, and the Fowles (as in Tom Fowle, Cassandra's doomed fiancé) at Kintbury in Berkshire, before Jane returned to Godmersham (where 'I shall eat Ice & drink French wine, & be above vulgar Economy'), via London.

A turning point came with the death of Edward Austen Knight's wife, Elizabeth. In the first instance, Edward sent two of his sons down to stay with their Aunt Jane in Southampton, while he dealt with the upheaval in his life. The motherless boys, Edward and George, arrived at the end of October 1808. '*They behave extremely* well in every respect,' Jane noted to Cassandra (who was at Godmersham, yet again), adding that 'We do not want amusement: bilbocatch, at which George is indefatigable, spillikins, paper ships, riddles, conundrums, and cards'.

Austen Knight followed up the dispatch of his children with a generous offer: either a house near Godmersham, or a property on the estate at Chawton, could be made available, rent-free, to his sisters and his mother. At once, the Austen women were given a new freedom. The pinched £450 *per annum* looked a lot brighter when there was no rent to pay. And while no one much wanted to live in Kent, the Hampshire house, with its pleasant setting and its six bedrooms, was very nearly ideal. However nice it was to live in the bosom of her family in Southampton, and away from the nullities of Bath, there was no escaping the fact that, at various times, Jane was sharing the house with brother Frank, his permanently pregnant wife Mary, sister Cassandra, Mrs Austen and the two great family friends, Mary and Martha Lloyd; as well as any other friends and associates who might be passing through. It would be a great luxury to retreat to somewhere quieter and less socially demanding. The name 'Chawton' comes up in the letters again and again, like an anticipated holiday.

By December, the move was being planned. 'Everybody,' said Jane, with something of her old vitality, 'is acquainted with Chawton & speaks of it as a remarkably pretty village; & everybody knows the House we describe – but nobody fixes on the right.' Mrs Austen stopped being ill for a while and began to acquire more silverware for the new home. And Jane would have her piano restored to her: 'Yes, yes, we *will* have a pianoforte, as good a one as can be got for thirty guineas, and I will practise country dances.' Her writing became infected with jauntiness – among the other notes about indispositions, bad weather and awkward visitors. She made, for example, a humorous defence of the card game speculation; she describes an attempt at making conversation with a man so deaf 'He could not hear a cannon, were it fired close to him'; and she made a big deal of her niece Fanny's critiques of her prose style, claiming that 'I begin already to weigh my words and sentences more than I did, and am looking about for a sentiment, an illustration or a metaphor in every corner of the room. Could my Ideas flow as fast as the rain in the Store closet it would be charming.' Even Mrs Austen's relapse into genteel invalidism suggested life returning to some kind of tolerable normality. 'For a day or two last week,' Jane wrote, fully inhabiting the role of the dutiful, unmarried daughter, 'my Mother was very poorly, with a return of *one* of her old complaints.'

Demob-happy, she rounded out her time by going to 'As many Balls as possible', and making her now-celebrated observation on Lady Sondes's forthcoming (and second) marriage: 'I consider everybody as having a right to marry *once* in their lives for love, if they can.' The apparent mellowness of this avowal is somewhat qualified by what comes next – 'And provided she will now leave off having bad headaches and being pathetic, I can allow her, I can *wish* her, to be happy.' But the sentiment is pure Austen: a cunningly wrought balance of worldly necessity versus the primacy of love; a concept which would serve her well in her fiction, as it turned out.

In April 1809, she left Southampton; by July, she was installed at Chawton. The change of situation evidently stirred her once more into thinking about life as a writer, and she fired off a letter to her fantastically dilatory publishers, Crosby & Co. (Cox had been dropped) who were still sitting on the *Northanger Abbey* manuscript from six years before, having done nothing whatsoever to publish it. Hiding behind the pseudonym 'Mrs Ashton Dennis', Jane wrote, 'I can only account for such an extraordinary circumstance by supposing the MS. by some carelessness to have been lost; & if that was the case, am willing to supply you with another copy if you are disposed to avail yourselves of it.' Crosby tersely replied that 'There was not any time stipulated for its publication, neither are we bound to publish it.' Moreover, if 'Mrs Ashton Dennis' tried to get it published anywhere else, 'We shall take proceedings to stop the sale.' Finally, 'The MS. shall be yours for the same we paid for it' – that is, she was welcome to buy it back off them for the same £10 they had originally paid her. They had reached an impasse.

So the Austens worked out another kind of routine, suitable for their new home. Mrs Austen perked up once again, and dedicated herself to vigorous gardening. According to Caroline Austen, a niece, Jane was put in charge of 'The tea and sugar stores . . . and the wine. And Cassandra did all the rest.' The two sisters, in the words of another niece, Anna Lefroy, 'Seemed to lead a life to themselves within the general family life which was shared only by each other.' The same niece – by this time a teenager, old enough to give a fairly trustworthy account – remembered her Aunt Jane as having a 'Figure tall and slight, but not drooping; well balanced, as was proved by her quick firm step. Her complexion of that rare sort which seems the particular property of light brunettes; a mottled skin, not fair but perfectly clear and healthy; the fine naturally curling hair, neither light nor dark; the bright hazel eyes to match, and the rather small, but well-shaped nose.'

Jane got up early, practised the piano, made breakfast, walked, visited, sewed. The house turned out to be both bucolic and connected to the world. Despite the rolling verdancy of its setting, Chawton was at a junction of the

main roads to the cities of London, Winchester, Southampton and Portsmouth, and traffic rattled past the house
continuously. The nearest place of any size was Alton,
halfway between a town and a large village, which lay a
walkable mile to the north, and supplied most of life's
necessities as well as having its own Assembly Room.
Edward Austen Knight's grand Chawton House was a
short walk to the south. The Austens were thus sequestered
but not isolated, placed at a comfortable distance from all
the locations central to Jane's Universe – London (where
Henry lived), Godmersham and Portsmouth. And, above
all, they were in Hampshire, their preferred county.

Jane Austen was clearly not a writer who needed to be
agitated into working. Regularity, continuity and a degree
of peacefulness were just right. After a while, she began to
feel that she might, Crosby notwithstanding, keep on at her
writing. We know this, because after two years at Chawton,
she had become a published author.

The first published novel was, as it turned out, *Sense and
Sensibility* – the *Elinor and Marianne* that Jane had started
around 1795. Having travelled with it through Bath and
Southampton, she disinterred it in the peace and quiet of
Chawton. She remodelled it, renamed it and gave it to
Henry Austen to sell in London. By April 1811, she was
staying with Henry at his address in Sloane Street in
London, and was correcting the proofs.

Who was the publisher, if not the egregious Crosby &
Co.? It turned out that Henry Austen had reached an
agreement with Thomas Egerton of the Military Library,
Whitehall. The deal was a conventional one by the

standards of the day: the author paid all the publishing costs, took all the sales receipts and paid the publisher a handling fee by way of commission. This meant that Jane had to put up between one- and two hundred pounds to get the book published in the first instance. This was money she clearly didn't have, and which she probably borrowed from Henry. She assumed that the book (and Henry) would make a loss, and very nobly tried to set aside some of her own diminutive income to meet that eventuality.

In fact, she made £140 from *Sense and Sensibility*, and the need to repay never arose. If this publishing deal sounds rather harshly speculative from the author's point of view, it was at least better than selling the copyright outright and losing all control over the book's progress, as had happened with Crosby and *Northanger Abbey*. A middle way did exist, in which a publisher might pay for the initial cost of the book and recoup his investment by taking a share of the proceeds. This would leave the author with anything from one-third to two-thirds of what was left – but this demanded a degree of confidence in the unpublished work, which Thomas Egerton clearly didn't possess.

So Jane was no worse off than many contemporary writers. The satisfaction of finding a publisher (at whatever price), of securing that kind of approval, of introducing that new hope into her life, made her write a letter of unusual ebullience to Cassandra, full of 'pleasure' and 'joy' in which everything was 'fresh & beautiful'. She was, in answer to Cassandra's enquiries, 'Never too busy to think of S & S. I can no more forget it, than a mother can forget her sucking child.' She was also 'Much gratified' by Mrs Knight's interest in the novel: 'I think she will like my Elinor, but cannot build on anything else.' Henry, fortunately, '*Has* hurried the Printer, & says he will see him again today,' which was as well, since 'I have scarcely a hope of its being out in June.' An elaborate party at Sloane Street saw Jane return to her old mock-flirtatiousness, where she describes herself being 'quite surrounded by acquaintance, especially Gentlemen; & what with Mr Hampson, Mr Seymour, Mr W. Knatchbull, Mr Guillemarde, Mr Cure, a Capt. Simpson, brother to *the* Capt. Simpson, besides Mr Walter and Mr Egerton, in addition to the Cookes & Miss Beckford & Miss Middleton, I had quite as much upon my hands as I could do.' Even the flowers in London had something going for them. 'Your Lilacs are in leaf,' she wrote, '*ours* are in bloom.' Then it went quiet again. And at some time, later in 1811, *Sense and Sensibility* was published.

Advertisements for the novel appeared in the late autumn, with the word 'interesting' attached: a euphemism indicating that the work was a piece of romantic fiction. By the end of the year, the book was released as *A Novel In Three Volumes* (to make it acceptable to the subscription libraries, who liked their books to be in highly lendable, subdivided formats), by 'A Lady'. Jane's anonymity was also in keeping with the times, and however keen she was for the book to sell, she was equally anxious to keep her identity hidden. At least one early reviewer, taking the title-page phrase 'Printed for the author' (as opposed to 'authoress') at face value, guessed that 'A Lady' was a man in disguise.

Not that it was unusual for a woman to write. Fanny Burney published *Evelina* in 1778 and *Camilla* in 1796, making a great success of what talents she possessed ('Good

Heaven, how did I start! The name struck my ear like a thunderbolt') and earning £3,000 from *Camilla* alone. Maria Edgeworth made so much money from her novels – between £1,500 and £2,000 a time – that she could support her numerous siblings in style ('A door opened', as it says in Miss Edgeworth's *Belinda*, 'and the macaw was heard to scream. "The macaw must go, Marriott, that is certain," said her ladyship, firmly'). But both authors were squeamish – certainly at the start of their careers – about seeing their names on the title page. There was something slightly improper about a woman, especially an unmarried woman, who wrote novels. It wasn't as bad as taking to the stage; but it was provocative, especially when one considers the noisy, highly coloured, populist fictional entertainments that flooded the market at the turn of the century, and which tainted the profession with sensationalism. The last thing Jane wanted was for people to take vulgar guesses at the real persons behind her fictional characters; or to force any kind of unwanted celebrity on her own family. And most of all, she didn't want people to assume that she was driven to write by poverty.

So Jane remained anonymous. The good news was that *Sense and Sensibility* was noticed just enough. The *Critical Review* liked the fact that its characters were plausible and its plotline in touch with reality. And it was 'Just long enough to interest without fatiguing.' The *British Critic* went further, after apologizing for the fact that it had tucked the review away in the back pages ('We think so favourably of this performance that it is with some reluctance we decline inserting it among our principal articles'), noting that 'The characters are happily delineated and admirably sustained' and that 'Nothing can be more happily pourtrayed than the picture of the elder brother'. It also noted that 'Not less excellent is the picture of the young lady of over exquisite sensibility, who falls immediately and violently in love with a male coquet, without listening to the judicious expostulations of her sensible sister.' In the end, 'We will, however, detain our female friends no longer than to assure them, that they may peruse these volumes not only with satisfaction but with real benefits, for they may learn from them, if they please, many sober and salutary maxims for the conduct of life, exemplified in a very pleasing and entertaining narrative.'

At the same time, members of high society were drawn to the book. One titled reader, Lady Bessborough, described *Sense and Sensibility* as 'A clever novel. They were full of it at Althorp' – Northampton home of the Spencer family – 'and though it ends stupidly I was much amused by it.' Princess Charlotte, fifteen-year-old daughter of the Prince Regent, came to the conclusion that it had been written by Lady Paget, read it, and wrote, '"Sence and Sencibility" I have *just finished* reading; it certainly is interesting, & you feel quite one of the company . . . I must say it interested me much.' Bit by bit, sales acquired momentum. The first print run of 750 copies sold out in eighteen months. A second edition appeared in 1813.

Sense and Sensibility is a long way from the formal perfections of Austen's later works; bits of it seem rushed or unfinished; it doesn't always make a lot of sense; there are slightly too many characters (Elizabeth Williams? Lucy Steele? Robert Ferrars?). And by the end, Marianne's pairing-off with Colonel Brandon may be convenient enough, but you don't hold out much hope for the relationship's long-term success; while Edward Ferrars looks much too furtive and underwhelming to keep Elinor happy. But among the workmanlike vulgarities of much Regency fiction, *Sense and Sensibility*, whatever its short-comings, must have seemed deeply refreshing. It made a modest, but perceptible, commercial impact – enough to encourage Thomas Egerton to buy the rights to *Pride and Prejudice* for £110. And it meant that Jane was a published author: not just an appendage to the rest of the family, but someone with a specific talent, a reason to be.

The image of Jane at work begins to take shape. At Chawton she practises the piano, first thing, before the others have got up: her musical tastes ranging from Handel, to Reginald Spofforth, Charles Dibdin and Domenico Cimarosa. She makes breakfast. She walks to Alton for provisions. And at some point in the day, she sits in the family living room at a small table near the window and commits herself to paper, at length, using a quill pen.

She writes – it would seem – on ordinary sheets of writing paper, folded in two. As she collects more and more of these tiny pamphlets, she stitches them together to make booklets, anticipating the novels they will finally become. She is a scrupulous reviser and reworker of her own material, amassing quantities of material, densely written and covered in hatchings and deletions. She describes herself as a miniaturist, working on a 'Little bit (two inches wide) of Ivory', with 'So fine a brush' – yet with all the industry of a Walter Scott or an Anthony Trollope.

Later on, a story will evolve that, reticent about her own work and keen to write without interference, she will wait for a particularly squeaky door to open – signalling the approach of another person – and take it as a signal to tuck her paperwork under the blotter, away from prying eyes. But would her manuscripts, even in small sections, have disappeared so conveniently out of view? To say nothing of the great wholesale revisions of *Elinor and Marianne* and *First Impressions*? It doesn't seem terribly plausible. If the image endures, it's because it expresses the sentimental affection we feel towards Miss Austen, the patient, un-lauded genius, ever-modest, ever-watchful.

And ever-productive. By November 1812, she has sold *Pride and Prejudice* to Thomas Egerton. A couple of months later, she is explaining to Cassandra that, having taken *First Impressions* in hand, she has 'Lop't and crop't so successfully . . . that I imagine it must be shorter than S. & S. altogether.' Her confidence is clearly growing. She has enough certainty in her own abilities to be ruthless with any material that dissatisfies her – 'lopping' and 'cropping' as she did – as well as enough self-belief to promote the finished product. She calls *Pride and Prejudice* 'My own darling child' and recounts how 'Miss Benn dined with us on the very day of the books coming & in the evening we set fairly at it, and read half the first vol. to her.' She also confesses a tender partiality to her fictional creation, Elizabeth Bennet, insisting that 'I think her as delightful a creature as ever appeared in print, and how I shall be able to tolerate those who do not like *her* at least I do not know.' And her status as a writer is manifested right in front of her, on the title page: no longer merely 'A Lady', she has become the 'Author of "Sense and Sensibility"'. She is a literary personage, and she finds it gratifying.

She also suffers the professional writer's passing agonies, revealing in her next letter to Cassandra (written in February 1813) that she has 'Had some fits of disgust' with the new book, not least because 'Our second evening's reading to Miss Benn had not pleased me so well, but I believe something must be attributed to my mother's too rapid way of getting on.' Much as she hates to blame her mother for mangling the text – 'She perfectly understands the characters herself' – tragically, 'She cannot speak as they ought.'

This leads her into what is for her, an almost self-indulgent essay on the book's merits. On the one hand, she writes to Cassandra that she is 'Quite vain enough and well satisfied enough' not to be bothered by criticism. On the other, 'The work is rather too light, and bright, and sparkling: it wants shade; it wants to be stretched out here and there with a long chapter of sense, if it could be had; if not, of solemn specious nonsense, about something unconnected with the story.' Jane chides herself, and at the same time, tries to make light of her own anxieties. So she turns the complaint into a joke, speculating that it would have been better to cram the thing with 'A critique on Walter Scott, or the history of Buonaparté, or anything that would form a contrast, and bring the reader with increased delight to the playfulness and epigrammatism of the general style.' But she still wants Cassandra to contradict her, to shout down her doubts and write back her approval – piquing her with a direct appeal: 'I doubt your quite agreeing with me here. I know your starched notions.' And then she allows herself a final piece of self-promotion: 'You must be prepared for the neighbourhood being perhaps already informed of there being such a Work in the World & in the Chawton World!' And then she manages to drop the subject.

She later indirectly comes back to this subject a few days later, when she vents her annoyance against 'Ladies who read those enormous great stupid quarto volumes which one always sees in the Breakfast parlour there' – 'there' being Manydown, where Cassandra was staying. Ostensibly acting in defence of a work by a certain Capt. Pasley, she sneers that the quarto-reading Ladies 'Must be acquainted with everything in the world. I detest a quarto.' In fact, Pasley's 'Book is too good for their society'. Well, what was Capt. Pasley to her? Other than a competent, energetic and above all, decently concise writer? One who, like Jane, got to the point? Her vigorous defence of the Captain is a further expression of the weight she now attaches to her own status as an author. Literary opinions are, for her, not just drawing-room pleasantries, but matters of deep significance.

The critics stirred themselves and took a look at *Pride and Prejudice*. The *New Review* mentioned it; the *Critical Review*, which had approved of her first novel, noted that 'The sentiments, which are dispersed over the work, do great credit to the *sense* and *sensibility* of the authoress.' Better, there was not 'One character which appears flat, or obtrudes itself upon the notice of the reader with troublesome impertinence.' The *British Critic* went further, claiming that *Pride and Prejudice* was not only 'Very far superior' to its rivals, but 'The story is well told, the characters remarkably well drawn and supported, and written with great spirit as well as vigour'. These qualities being precisely the qualities, oddly enough, which Jane so admired in Capt. Pasley's writing. The only shortcoming, in the eyes of the *British Critic*, was that 'The story has no great variety.'

Perhaps not. But the characters do. Indeed, *Pride and Prejudice* is generally taken to be Jane Austen's personal favourite among all her novels, not least because of Elizabeth Bennet, an author-surrogate if ever there was one; and Mr Darcy, so perversely appealing that his character has become a cultural icon (or convenient shorthand for the sensual brooding British male) in the two hundred years since the novel was published.

You can see Jane's continuing faith in her creation in a July 1813 letter to brother Frank Austen in which she announced that every copy of *Sense and Sensibility* had been sold. As well as being rightly proud of her new earning power ('I have now therefore written myself into £250 – which only makes me long for more'), she intimated that work has started on her next novel – 'I have something in hand' – and which 'I hope on the credit of P. & P. will sell well, tho' not half so entertaining.' Since this next novel would turn out to be the mildly problematic *Mansfield Park*, she was probably right to assume that the book would need all the help it could get from *Pride and Prejudice* in order to make any commercial headway.

She was also right in that *none* of her subsequent novels would be as purely entertaining as *Pride and Prejudice*. Structurally, the book can creak occasionally; and that

Johnsonian antithesis (in which contradictory ideas are balanced or contrasted in a parallel structure), central to the plot, is probably getting to the end of its usefulness. But the characters are wonderful – not just the key players in the comic romance, but the supporting cast, too: Mr Bennet, Mr Collins, Lady Catherine de Bourgh. Added to which, Miss Austen's prose style has settled, becoming that note-perfect balance of spaciousness and compression, of surface and interior, which sometimes deceives the eye, but never the ear. This combination then gives us at least two unequivocally celebrated moments in literature: 'It is a truth universally acknowledged, that a single man in possession of a good fortune, must be in want of a wife' – arguably the best-known opening line of any English novel; and the moment when Elizabeth first feasts her gaze on Pemberley, Darcy's country estate – 'She had never seen a place for which nature had done more, or where natural beauty had been so little counteracted by an awkward taste. They were all of them warm in their admiration; and at that moment she felt, that to be mistress of Pemberley might be something!'

And there is also the truth, universally acknowledged, that *Pride and Prejudice* is a great comic romance, with its yearnings and its formalities, its passions and its inhibitions, all wrapped in the straitjacketed social conventions of the day and delivered in Jane's sharp, unsentimental, incredibly deft, authorial voice. The novel is infinitely more than a Regency romantic-comedy, or a slice of off-the-shelf romantic fiction – and miles removed from the steamings and exclaimings of a novelist such as Fanny Burney. Miss Austen's dryness, her refusal to be anything other than grown-up and her passion for mockery mean that when the love dilemmas are finally resolved, everything feels as if it has been earned. Although the reader can see the end coming a mile off, it is nevertheless perfectly satisfying when it does arrive.

While waiting for *Pride and Prejudice* to add lustre to her reputation, Jane went back to London in September 1813, to visit brother Henry. London was now no longer the scene of 'Dissipation and vice' it used to be, and she spent her time shopping, theatre-going and visiting exhibitions. She also had to cope with Henry's tiresome indiscretions about *Pride and Prejudice*: 'Lady Robert is delighted with P. and P., and really *was* so, as I understand, before she knew who wrote it, for, of course, she knows now. He told her with as much satisfaction as if it were my wish.' A few days after that she comments to her brother Frank:

> Henry heard P. & P. warmly praised in Scotland, by Lady Robt Kerr & another Lady; – & what does he do in the warmth of his Brotherly vanity & Love, but immediately tell them who wrote it! A Thing once set going in that way – one knows how it spreads! – and he, dear Creature, has set it going so much more than once.

Her scandalized tone was only partly authentic. Another part of her was much more resigned about the whole problem of maintaining her anonymity, even seeing mercenary possibilities in the situation: 'The truth is that the Secret has spread so far as to be scarcely the Shadow of a secret now – & that I beleive whenever the 3d' – novel, presumably – 'appears, I shall not even attempt to tell Lies about it. – I shall rather try to make all the Money than all the Mystery I can of it. – People shall pay for their knowledge if I can make them.'

It was an intriguing position to be in. Jane was now reaching the height of her powers. *Pride and Prejudice* was in the process of becoming her most successful novel, with the first edition of around 1,500 copies selling out in mid-summer, 1813, a second edition appearing in the autumn and a third edition a few years after that. It also confirmed her currency – although not always her popularity – with the 'smart set'. The future wife of the poet Lord Byron (Lady Byron), the current Lady Davy (the wife of poet, chemist and inventor Sir Humphrey Davy), Warren Hastings (former Governor-General of India) and Irish authors Maria Edgeworth and Richard Brinsley Sheridan all passed judgement on the work – some favourable, some less so. At the same time, a nice worldliness infused Jane's letters, with their busy references to Lady Bridges (brother Edward's mother-in-law), the King of Sweden, the Knatchbulls, the Wigram family, the amusing Mr D'Arblay, Chilham Castle in Kent, William Hammond ('The only young man of renown'), Lady Honeywood, the Plumptre family, the actor Edmund Kean, Covent Garden in central London; and their abrupt, almost Wildean put-downs – 'There is nobody Brilliant nowadays'; 'How can people pretend to be fashionable or to bathe out of England!'; 'He talks too much & is conceited – besides having a vulgarly shaped mouth.'

In between London visits, she went to Godmersham to be slightly more in the bosom of her family, and play the role of clever Aunt Jane. She had numerous nephews and nieces, some to her liking, some too boisterous and dull to be much fun ('Edward is no Enthusiast in the beauties of Nature. His Enthusiasm is for the sports of the field only'). A clear favourite, though, was Fanny Knight, aged twenty in the year of *Pride and Prejudice*'s publication, and an increasing presence in Jane's letters.

By the start of November, Jane was enjoying Godmersham's luxuries, 'Very snug, in my own room, lovely morning, excellent fire, fancy me', having spent the previous day finding 'Many Douceurs in being a sort of Chaperon for I am put on the Sofa near the Fire & can drink as much wine as I like.' A little concert of music had been put on in the evening, where Fanny Knight had played, and Lady Bridges had 'Found me handsomer than she expected, so you see I am not so very bad as you might think for'. And then, in the new year of 1814, she was back in London, complaining – in an echo of the older, money-conscious Jane, rather than the newer, socially smart Jane – about the dismal workmanship of the people who dyed her clothing: 'What wicked people dyers are. They begin with dipping their souls in scarlet sin.' Her way of life had changed; but it hadn't changed entirely.

For much of the time, though, she was working on her first complete new book for ten years: *Mansfield Park*. She probably made a start on it in early 1811; by mid-1813, it was finished. Egerton published it in 1814 as a novel 'By the author of "Sense and Sensibility" and "Pride and Prejudice"'. However much movement there might have been from Chawton to Godmersham to London, Miss

Austen kept up her schedule of – roughly – a book a year; and would do so until she died.

Which meant that by March 1814, she was taking understandable pleasure in the fact that 'Henry has finished Mansfield Park, & his approbation has not lessened. He found the last half of the last volume *extremely interesting*.' And by June, her friends The Revd Samuel and Mrs Cooke, were also fans – the Revd Cooke reckoning the novel 'The most sensible he ever read', while 'The manner in which I treat the clergy delights them very much.' The problem was that, however pleasing the comments, they were partial, coming from friends and family. The professional reviewers, worryingly, didn't touch *Mansfield Park*. Indeed, the only appraisals it received were by word of mouth, or in private letters.

Mansfield Park is a trickier proposition than *Pride and Prejudice*, there's no doubting it. A properly mature novel, it does far less to ingratiate itself with the reader than its predecessors. Fanny Price, the heroine, is both stoical and a wet blanket ('In excessive trembling she was enduring all these fearful thoughts'), while the rest of the cast is mostly a *galère* of layabouts, flirts and scolds, with only the saintly Edmund Bertram to raise the tone. It takes longer to unpack its story than either *Sense and Sensibility* or *Pride and Prejudice*, with consequent demands on the reader's patience (but with consequent rewards, too). It's not in the least a comedy romance – instead, it's a relatively sombre tale, illuminated with knowing humour. And it pursues a sternly moral argument, from start to finish. The naughtiness of the Bertram children and their friends – the Crawfords, Mr Yates – is brilliantly observed, highly entertaining and pointedly unedifying ('You will not refuse to visit me in prison?' wheedles the sleazy Henry Crawford to Julia Bertram, 'I think I see you coming with your basket'). And the evolving tenderness between Fanny Price and Edmund Bertram ('As for Edmund, she could neither speak, nor look, nor think, when the last moment came with *him*') offers none of the satisfactions of Elizabeth Bennet's taming of Mr Darcy. It is, in other words, an ambitious production, and one that – unfairly – carries the label *difficult*.

Mansfield Park divides readers today, and it divided readers in 1814. There were plenty of people – other than brother Henry and the Revd Cooke – who found things to admire. The Earl of Dudley was a quiet enthusiast, as was Maria Edgeworth ('We have been much entertained with *Mansfield Park*'). Lady Robert Kerr, the fan of *Pride and Prejudice*, claimed that *Mansfield Park* was 'Universally admired in Edinburgh, by all the *wise ones*.' Lady Vernon, on the other hand, thought it 'Not much of a novel', although 'very natural'. And Thomas Egerton, despite selling out the first edition by the end of the year, had so little faith in it that he refused to print a second edition. John Murray then picked up the title, and just over a year later, did produce a second edition, running to 1,750 copies. But even then, he wouldn't go so far as to insist on putting a review of the novel in his own *Quarterly Review*. This must have been unnerving for Jane. Hoping to build on the solid success of *Pride and Prejudice*, she found her apprehensions about *Mansfield Park* justified as the first fully realized work of her mature years failed to overwhelm its readership.

* * *

An unintended consequence of all this was that Jane's relations started to solicit her views on their *own* literary productions. Anna Austen was the daughter of brother James the cleric – an essayist and poet in his own right – and had, from an early age, shown a talent for storytelling. Now aged twenty, she wrote a novella entitled *Which Is The Heroine?* and sent it to Jane – who liked the title 'Very well, & I dare say shall grow to like it very much in time'. However flattering it was to be consulted, it also proved to be a challenge to her capacity for tactfulness.

Many of Jane's comments on the novella were strictly editorial in nature and concerned, for example, the etiquette of formal introductions, the occasional misnaming of the county of Devon or a continuity problem involving a broken arm. Elsewhere there are more personal judgements – 'I should like to have had more of Devereux. I do not feel enough acquainted with him'; or, 'I do not like a Lover's speaking in the 3d person; – it is too much like the formal part of Lord Orville, & I think is not natural. If *you* think differently however, you need not mind me.' Or, more seriously, 'I have a good many criticisms to make – more than you will like.'

At the same time, these corrections and admonishments justified the encouragements which, elsewhere, Jane heaped on *Which Is The Heroine?* She declared that the work 'Has entertained me extremely, all of us indeed'; that 'I am impatient for more'; that 'We are all very much amused, & like the work quite as well as ever'; and that 'You are now collecting your People delightfully, getting them exactly into such a spot as is the delight of my life.' The sheer conscientiousness of her replies, spread over numerous letters, bespoke the affection she felt for her young relative.

She also gave advice on the real world to Fanny Knight, her sweet, fair-haired young niece (if Cassandra's water-colour of her is to be believed) who had not only engaged Jane's sympathies, but more recently those of a young man called John Plumtre.

Plumtre was a problem: Fanny encouraged him during the summer of 1814, before changing her mind in the autumn of the same year. What should she do? 'I have no scruple in saying you cannot be in Love,' Aunt Jane observed, right at the start of a long letter written in mid-November. Since Fanny's original letter to Jane no longer exists, Jane's half of the dialogue inevitably drags the reader into a world of teasing inferences. 'It seems as if your being secure of him (as you say yourself) had made you Indifferent', is transparent enough. But she then writes that 'There was a little disgust I suspect, at the Races – & I do not wonder at it. His expressions there would not do for one who had rather more Acuteness, Penetration & Taste, than Love, which was your case.' And yet, on the positive side, she writes that Plumtre is, 'just what he ever was, only more evidently & uniformly devoted to *you*'. Indeed, 'My dear Fanny, the more I write about him, the warmer my feelings become, the more strongly I feel the sterling worth of such a young Man & the desirableness of your growing in love with him again. I recommend this most thoroughly.' A page later, though, she writes:

Having written so much on one side of the question, I shall turn round & entreat you not to commit yourself farther, & not to think of accepting him unless you really do like him. Anything is to be preferred or endured rather than marrying without Affection; and if his deficiencies of Manner &c &c strike you more than all his good qualities. If you continue to think strongly of them, give him up at once.

What, exactly, is Jane's agenda, here? Does she see her job as one of tidying up Fanny's lines of argument and presenting them back to her so that she and only she can make up her own mind in a more orderly and rational way ('As to Opinion or Counsel I am sure none will [be] extracted worth having from this letter')? Is it really an attempt to wean her off 'Poor dear Mr J. P.!' by rehearsing such arguments as were, more or less, in his favour – his 'Strict principles', his 'Modesty', his tendency towards 'Becoming even Evangelical'? And by itemizing these dull attractions, by setting down his ambiguous worth in black and white, thus attempting subterfuge to put her niece off?

Or is Jane – far from offering much wise counsel to Fanny – the plaything of her own emotions? As she put it, 'I am feeling differently every moment, & shall not be able to suggest a single thing can assist your Mind.' A sense of loss, or potential loss, informs the next pages; it's impossible not to hear the nostalgia of the unmarried, nearly forty-year-old, spinster aunt, when she writes of how 'He was the *first* young Man who attached himself to you. That was the charm, & most powerful it is.' And again, when she counsels her niece to be realistic, above all things:

There *are* such beings in the World, perhaps, one in a Thousand, as the Creature You and I should think perfection, Where Grace & Spirit are united to Worth, where the Manners are equal to the Heart & Understanding, but such a person may not come in your way, or if he does, he may not be the eldest son of a Man of Fortune, the Brother of your particular friend, & belonging to your own County.

She then adds: 'Think of all this Fanny. Mr J. P. – has advantages which do not often meet in one person.' She sounds almost stricken at the prospect. And yet the counter-argument, when it does arrive – 'Anything is to be preferred or endured rather than marrying without Affection' – could easily be taken as a hurried recapitulation of the long night in which Jane decided to reject Harris Bigg Wither.

Indeed, her final and settled opinion seems to emerge a week or so later when she writes, 'I cannot wish you with your present very cool feelings to devote yourself in honour to him.' She then compounds her position with a sober admonition: 'Nothing can be compared to the misery of being bound *without* Love, bound to one, & preferring another. *That* is a Punishment which you do *not* deserve.' How could Jane be so sure? No one in her immediate family was in the punishing position she describes, not even brother James, whose second marriage – to Mary Lloyd – had sometimes proved problematic. Her opinion is almost luxurious in its certainty, as if it were one of the few indulgences a spinster could afford.

Nevertheless Fanny Knight let the relationship continue, aimlessly, before John Plumtre finally got dismissed in 1817. She then turned without enthusiasm to another suitor, a Mr Wildman, before asking Jane *again* what she thought of the match. Fanny was in an importuning mood, as well as being 'Nervous and apt to cry', but Jane was too besotted with her to offer much constructive thought. 'Who can keep pace with the fluctuations of your Fancy, the Capprizios of your Taste, the Contradictions of your Feelings?' she demanded of 'The delight of my Life'. Fanny could 'Hardly think what a pleasure it is to me, to have such thorough pictures of your Heart'. She was worth her 'Weight in Gold.' And as for marriage? The answer was still clear enough. 'Oh! what a loss it will be when you are married'; and, 'I shall hate you when your delicious play of Mind is all settled down into conjugal & maternal affections.' In short, Fanny should drop Mr Wildman. He wasn't good enough for her – except 'All that I urge against him will rather make you take his part more, sweet perverse Fanny.'

As it turned out, Fanny decided to drop Mr Wildman, marrying instead Sir Edward Knatchbull, Bart., three years after Jane's death. In 1869 she then won the detestation of generations of Jane Austen's fans by writing that her Aunt 'Was not so refined as she ought to have been from her talent'; the Austens were nothing more than 'Mediocre'; both Cassandra and Jane, were 'Very much below par as to good Society and its ways'. Even allowing for the necessary grim *hauteur* of a socially important family in High Victorian England, this seems a shabby repayment for Aunt Jane's love and attention. Unless, of course, she felt embarrassed by it, five decades later.

Jane closed one of her letters to Fanny (written in November, 1814) with the news that 'The first Edit: of

M. P. is all sold. – Your Uncle Henry is rather wanting me to come to Town, to settle about a 2d Edit:'. In a subsequent letter, she wrote, more resignedly, 'It is not settled yet whether I *do* hazard a 2d Edition. We are to see Egerton today, when it will probably be determined. – People are more ready to borrow & praise, than to buy – which I cannot wonder at; – but tho' I like praise as well as anybody, I like what Edward calls *Pewter* too.' Whatever else happened, the business of writing had to go on.

By October 1815, she had written *Emma*, her master-piece, and was in talks with John Murray about publication. Inevitably, dealing with yet another hard-nosed London publisher was deeply unsatisfactory. Murray offered £450 for *Emma*, but wanted the copyrights to *Mansfield Park* and *Sense And Sensibility* thrown in. 'He is a rogue of course, but a civil one', Jane observed wearily, adding, 'It will end in my publishing for myself I daresay.' (Which was how it turned out: Murray published at the author's expense, and gave the profits to her after he had taken his commission). A month later, and Jane felt Murray was wasting time over the actual publication. Brother Henry, who normally took a hand in these matters, was unwell, so it fell to Jane to grumble to the dilatory Murray. 'I am so very much disappointed and vexed by the delays of the printers,' she wrote to him, 'that I cannot help begging to know whether there is no hope of their being quickened. Instead of the work being ready by the end of the present month, it will hardly, at the rate we now proceed, be finished by the end of next.'

But for once, she had a secret ally to call on. It was the Prince Regent. It might seem unlikely, but retiring, percipient Aunt Jane had a fan in the fat voluptuary who was the Prince Regent. A mutual (and well-connected) medical acquaintance let it be known that the Prince 'often read' Jane's novels, and 'had a set in each of his residences'. Moreover, on the Prince's personal and specific instruction, the Revd James Stanier Clarke, Librarian of Carlton House – which had been the Prince's London residence since the end of the eighteenth century – came and paid court to Miss Austen. He then invited her to pay court to *him* in Carlton House; which she did, on 13 November 1815. Jane returned to Hans Place, off Sloane Street, where she was staying with the (still ill) Henry. From here she wrote to Mr Clarke, asking whether she was indeed now expected to dedicate her new work, *Emma*, to the Prince Regent. 'As I am very anxious to be quite certain of what was intended,' she noted, 'I entreat you to have the goodness to inform me how such a Permission is to be understood, & whether it is incumbent on me to shew my sense of the Honour, by inscribing the Work now in the Press, to H.R.H.' She then added, just to be perfectly sure, 'I shd be equally concerned to appear either Presumptuous or Ungrateful.'

Well, the Prince did want a dedication. Clarke wrote back by return of post, 'It is certainly not *incumbent* on you to dedicate your work now in the Press to His Royal Highness; but if you wish to do the Regent that honour either now or at any future period, I am happy to send you that permission which need not require any more trouble or solicitation on your Part.' It was a great honour. The only question is whether Jane really wanted to be associated quite so closely with His Royal Highness. After all, he was known less for his personal charm and exquisite sensibilities (which he did possess, despite everything), and more for his sexual incontinence, crudely selfish appetites and colossal financial irresponsibility. He had almost single-handedly reduced the Monarchy to an object of scorn, and was mocked in public and in private. The Regent may have 'Read & admired' all Jane's publications, but he was an embarrassment.

And Miss Austen's particular take on him? Apart from one or two indirectly snide references to him in the letters, anything of Jane's attitude to the Prince has to be inferred from whatever else one knows about her. Decently pious – with some Evangelical leanings, and therefore an extra sense of personal witness – a spinster, and a woman of limited financial resources, she was, in her own person, pretty much the Prince's diametric opposite. In her writings, she naturally espouses good governance and chaste sensibilities while opprobriating vanity, self-indulgence and moral laxity. The obvious conclusion is that she would have deeply disliked just about everything the Prince stood for.

And yet a nod from the Royal Family was better than no nod from the Royal Family – not least because it enabled Jane to put some pressure on her publisher. In the same letter in which she grumbled about the slowness of *Emma*'s printers, she asked John Murray whether it would be 'likely that the printers will be influenced to greater dispatch and punctuality by knowing that the work is to be dedicated, by permission, to the Prince Regent? If you can make that circumstance operate, I shall be very glad.' Naturally, it worked. Murray suddenly woke up and wrote ingratiatingly back the next day. As Jane then explained to Cassandra:

'He is so very polite indeed, that it is quite overcoming. – The Printers have been waiting for Paper – the blame is thrown upon the Stationer – but he gives his word that I shall have no farther cause for dissatisfaction.' And a couple of days after that, 'The Printers continue to supply me very well.' So there was *some* merit in being a favourite of the Prince.

On the other hand, she still had the Revd James Stanier Clarke to deal with. He evidently found Miss Austen rather bewitching. Having explained to her that the Prince's approval was a matter of course, he went on to express his own particular enthusiasm, noting that 'Your late Works, Madam, and in particular *Mansfield Park* reflect the highest honour on your Genius & your Principles,' and that 'in every new work your mind seems to increase its energy and powers of discrimination.' Given that every writer wishes to be praised for his or her most recent accomplishment – rather than a favourite from a few years back – these were welcome words. But Clarke didn't stop there. He felt intimate enough with Jane ('Dear Madam') to be 'Allowed to ask you, to delineate in some future Work the Habits of Life and Character and enthusiasm of a Clergyman – who should pass his time between the metropolis & the Country.' Apparently, no contemporary writer had 'In my mind quite delineated an English Clergyman, at least of the present day' – a Clergyman surprisingly like Clarke himself, 'Silent when glad, affectionate tho' shy', as well as, 'Fond of, & entirely engaged in Literature – no man's Enemy but his own.' He rounded off the suggestion with a compelling, 'Pray dear Madam think of these things', before adding a P. S. to the effect that he was off to

Sevenoaks, 'But hope on my return to have the honour of seeing you again.'

It's not entirely clear whether Miss Austen's appeal was personal and feminine, or professional and literary – to have your life written by Jane Austen would be quite a vanity project, after all – or whether it was a mixture of the two. Nor is it clear whether Clarke was a genuine admirer of Jane's, who just wanted to find a way into her heart; or whether he was a real-life Mr Collins, helplessly blinkered and self-important and vain. She, on the other hand, didn't want to have much to do with him; but she didn't want to offend him, either. She wrote him a long and quite candid letter in December 1815, in which she thanked him for his praise of her earlier works, confessing that 'I am too vain to wish to convince you that you have praised them beyond their merits.' She was also keen to make known her nervousness about *Emma*, and expressed her anxiety 'That this fourth work should not disgrace what was good in the others.' In fact, she was more than anxious. She was 'Very strongly haunted with the idea that to those readers who have preferred "Pride and Prejudice" it will appear inferior in wit, and to those who have preferred "Mansfield Park" very inferior in good sense.'

She responded to the tricky subject of whether or not to start a novel based around a character like the Revd Clarke's with deftness: 'I am quite honoured by your thinking me capable of drawing such a clergyman as you have the sketch of in your note of Nov. 16th. But I assure you I am *not*.' Reasons why not included an ability to write comic characters, but not serious or virtuous ones; insufficient knowledge of manly things such as science and philosophy; and a lack of familiarity with the Classics (or at least English Literature), the meat and drink of any cultured clergyman's discourse. 'I think I may boast myself to be,' she concluded in a flourish, 'with all possible vanity, the most unlearned and uninformed female who ever dared to be an authoress.'

Mr Clarke wrote back an even longer letter in reply, revealing a successful trip to Sevenoaks, a forthcoming trip to the Egremonts at Petworth ('Where your Praises have long been sounded as they ought to be') and an absolute refusal to give up the idea of having a novel written about him. He urged Jane to keep the idea warm, have her friends help out with their own reminiscences of other clergymen ('Memoires pour servir – as the French term it'), while allowing her some latitude, nonetheless, in the prosecution of her art ('Do let us have an English Clergyman after *your* fancy'). More details follow from his own life (having to bury his own mother; disapproval of tithes), after which, a playful apology for importuning Miss Austen, and, last of all, an open invitation to make free with a little place he has in Golden Square ('There is a small Library there much at your Service').

March 1816 sees him pestering her yet again, first with the news that the Prince Regent has just appointed him 'Chaplain and Private English Secretary to the Prince of Cobourg'; secondly, with the hint that 'When you again appear in print you may chuse to dedicate your volumes to Prince Leopold: any historical romance, illustrative of the history of the august House of Cobourg, would just now be very interesting.' Jane's response? After duly congratulating the incredible Revd Clarke on his promotion, Jane wrote that 'I am fully sensible that an historical romance, founded on the House of Saxe Cobourg, might be much more to the purpose of profit or popularity than such pictures of domestic life in country villages as I deal in. But I could no more write a romance than an epic poem.' And, just in case that wasn't definitive enough, she reinforced her position: 'I must keep to my own style and go on in my own way; and though I may never succeed again in that, I am convinced that I should totally fail in any other.'

The surprising thing is that she then *did* contemplate a novel in which the Revd Clarke's suggestions would be put to good use. Or, more accurately, she sketched out some notes towards a spoof, a parody of sensationalist fiction, centring around a clergyman, his daughter, a thwarted hero, a preposterous villain and numerous staggering misadventures. Called merely *Plan of a Novel*, it was written in amused haste in 1816. The character of the clergyman is curiously familiar: an exemplary individual, a lover of literature, a detester of tithes, a man who may have buried his own mother. As 'Nobody's enemy but his own', he finds himself, after a terrible series of reversals, in Kamchatka of all places, with his shattered daughter, where, 'Quite worn down, finding his end approaching, throws himself on the Ground, and after 4 or 5 hours of tender advice and parental Admonition to his miserable Child, expires in a fine burst of Literary Enthusiasm, intermingled with Invectives against holders of Tithes.' One can only guess at the caustic pleasure Jane must have felt when she wrote it.

In the end, *Plan of a Novel* was an interesting enough distraction from the real locus of Jane's anxieties: *Emma*. She wrote at the end of *Plan of a Novel*, that 'the name of the work *not* to be *Emma*, but of the same sort as *S. & S.* and *P. & P.*', indicating that, whatever its merits, *Emma* was not likely to enjoy the same easy ride as its predecessors.

Part of *Emma*'s greatness, of course, lies in the fact that it doesn't yield its rewards easily. It's demanding, and, really, it demands to be read fairly slowly. Only then do its stateliness and architectural quality start to make sense. With some work from the reader, that very Jane Austen sensation of completeness without excess – the feeling that even though *Emma* is a longish book, you couldn't add a word or take one away (especially from the wonderfully subtle dialogue) – begins to emerge.

One of the big problems with *Emma* – and, at the same time, one of the things key to its stature as a novel – lies with the characters. Jane was famously supposed to have said, 'I am going to take a heroine whom no one but myself will much like', and the resulting character, Emma Woodhouse, is not an easy person to get on with. Rich, beautiful, unattached, clever, snobbish and judgemental, she spends a considerable portion of the book getting things wrong. This is true whether it involves her dismissal of the innocent farmer, Mr Martin – 'I had no idea that he could be so very clownish, so totally without air. I had imagined him, I confess, a degree or two nearer gentility'; or her excessive enthusiasm for Mr Frank Churchill – 'She felt immediately that she should like him; and there was a well-bred ease of manner, and a readiness to talk, which convinced her that he came intending to be acquainted with her, and that acquainted they soon must be.' But Emma Woodhouse is also terribly compelling: the energy of the book springs from her and her half-baked schemes; she is irrepressible and wrong-headed, and her character combines wit and silliness in a way which is more sophisticated and more acutely observed than anything that could be achieved in the formal moralities of *Pride and Prejudice* or *Mansfield Park*.

The other characters pose their own problems, too. Mr Knightley, although earmarked for romantic happiness, can seem stuffy – even in comparison with his forerunner, Mr Darcy – and Emma's ridiculous Milquetoast father ('You and I will have a nice basin of gruel together') manages to be both comic and deeply irritating. The fact that Emma will persist in showing him all kinds of tender solicitudes only makes it worse. The character of Harriet Smith has too much of the Fanny Price about her to be truly sympathetic. And Jane Fairfax, although full of significance, doesn't quite occupy enough of the centre stage. And so on. *Emma* is not a blithe novel, and its cast of characters reflects this. But it is, in all probability, Jane Austen's finest work, and has a reasonable claim to be considered the first truly great English novel.

Although advertised for publication in December of 1815, and now boasting its smart dedication to the Prince Regent 'By his Royal Highness's Dutiful and Obedient Humble Servant, The Author', it took a while for *Emma* to make its way into the public consciousness. The Countess of Morley had an early copy, and wrote to Jane that 'I am already become intimate in the Woodhouse family, & feel that they will not amuse & interest me less than the Bennetts, Bertrams, Noriss & all their admirable predecessors – I *can* give them no higher praise.' To which Jane replied, 'In my present state of doubt as to her reception in the World, it is particularly gratifying to me to receive so early an assurance of your Ladyship's approbation.' She was ambitious for the book to succeed, but, filled with self-doubt, was also desperate to 'Believe that I have not yet – as almost every Writer of Fancy does sooner or later – overwritten myself.'

After that there was an anxious lull. Months went by before *Emma* was at last given space in an assortment of journals – *The Augustan Review, Monthly Review, The Gentleman's Magazine, Literary Panorama*. The critics pronounced: The *Monthly Review* called *Emma* a 'Harmless amusement'; the *British Critic* allowed that 'It rarely happens that in a production of this nature we have so little to find fault with'; and according to *The Gentleman's Magazine*, 'If *Emma* be not allowed to rank in the very highest class of modern novels, it certainly may claim at least a distinguished degree of eminence in that species of composition. It is amusing, if not instructive; and has no tendency to deteriorate the heart.'

Elsewhere, phrases such as 'Inoffensive and well principled' and 'We are not less inclined to speak well of this tale', were bandied about. Within the family itself, the Leigh Perrots 'Saw many beauties' in *Emma*, but preferred *Pride and Prejudice* – 'Darcy and Elizabeth had spoilt them for anything else', while nice Anna 'Preferred Emma to all the heroines'. All in all, the critical response was all right, but not much more than that; and it would have remained that way, had it not been for Sir Walter Scott.

Scott was also published by John Murray, and Murray leaned on him to give *Emma* a good write-up in the

Quarterly Review. Which he duly did. The review appeared in March 1816, and displayed – to Scott's eternal credit – the greatest sympathy with Jane's artistic vision. He had been praised for his sense of naturalism in *Waverley* (1814), and made it clear how much he approved of the new trend in novel-writing, with its 'Art of copying from nature as she really exists in the common walks of life, and presenting to the reader, instead of the splendid scenes of an imaginary world, a correct and striking representation of that which is daily taking place around him.' He went on to note how difficult it was to get this kind of fiction right, and that 'Something more than a mere sign-post likeness is also demanded. The portrait must have spirit and character, as well as resemblance.' His verdict on the novel? That it was a good one:

> We, therefore, bestow no mean compliment upon the author of *Emma*, when we say that, keeping close to common incidents, and to such characters as occupy the ordinary walks of life, she has produced sketches of such spirit and originality, that we never miss the excitation which depends upon a narrative of uncommon events, arising from the consideration of minds, manners and sentiments, greatly above our own. In this class she stands almost alone.

In fact, 'The author's knowledge of the world, and the peculiar tact with which she presents characters that the reader cannot fail to recognize, reminds us something of the merits of the Flemish school of painting. The subjects are not often elegant, and certainly never grand; but they are finished up to nature, and with a precision which delights the reader.' It was a long review, and a heartfelt one, and one of the earliest and best appreciations of Jane's talent – from a writer at the absolute peak of his own celebrity.

Not that Jane knew who had written the review. She was a fan of Scott's, and had confessed as much to niece Anna, a few years earlier: 'Walter Scott has no business to write novels, especially good ones. – It is not fair. – He has Fame and Profit enough as a Poet, and should not be taking the bread out of other people's mouths'; what's more, she did not 'Mean to like "Waverley" if I can help it – but fear I must.' But did she sense Scott's hand behind the praise in the *Quarterly Review*? If she did, she was too bound up with the success of *Emma* to say so.

Instead, she fretted, obsessing gloomily over what was absent. 'The Authoress of "Emma",' she wrote to John Murray, with regard to the *Quarterly Review*, 'has no reason, I think, to complain of her treatment in it, except in the total omission of "Mansfield Park." I cannot but be sorry that so clever a man as the Reviewer of "Emma" should consider it as unworthy of being noticed.' *Emma* was terribly important to her, and her anxiety for the book coloured everything else. Sales were slow, and however much James Stanier Clarke reassured her that the novel was 'Excellent', and that the Prince Regent's circle had paid her 'The just tribute of their praise', she wanted the book to make a real impact with the larger reading public. It didn't.

She was also bowed by other concerns. Henry Austen had co-founded a London bank – Austen, Maunde & Tilson –

early in the century, had over-reached himself and, with the end of the Napoleonic Wars and the economic contraction that followed, went bankrupt at the start of 1816. This, on top of months of debilitating illness. His crash not only wiped him out, but threatened the finances of Uncle James Leigh Perrot and brother Edward Knight, Jane's benevolent landlord. For all his imprudence, occasional asininity and, now, recklessness with the financial well-being of the whole Austen family, Henry was dear to Jane. He had done his best to help her literary career and had always been affectionate, and the crash upset her. Thus, any good news concerning him ('Henry does not write diffusely, but chearfully'; 'We think Uncle Henry in excellent Looks') was passed on with a note of relief; as was confirmation of the fact that, in a final roll of the dice, Henry had taken Holy Orders, with a view to seeing out his days in tranquillity as a clergyman.

But Jane herself was starting to fail. Her letters – still implacably amusing and gossipy when writing to Cassandra and her nephews and nieces (at least two of whom were turning their hands to writing fiction) – nonetheless start to contain glancing references to an ailment. 'Thank you,' she says to Cassandra, and then continues:

> ... my Back has given me scarcely any pain for many days. – I have an idea that agitation does it as much harm as fatigue, & that I was ill at the time of your going, from the very circumstance of your going. – I am nursing myself up now into as beautiful a state as I can, because I hear that Dr White means to call on me before he leaves the Country.

She then writes to her nephew, James Edward, with regard
to a proposed dinner with Uncle Charles Austen, 'I was
forced to decline it, the walk is beyond my strength (though
I am otherwise very well)'. And this from the great walker
Aunt Jane.

It seems that she took the waters at Cheltenham Spa, to
find some relief. When she felt particularly bad, she
stretched herself out on three hard chairs, leaving the sofa
for her mother. The complaint came and went. As well as
back pains and fatigue, she experienced fever, faintness, a
'discharge' as well as some kind of gastric disorder.
Informed guesses have concluded that it was a recurrence
of the 'putrid fever' she caught as a pupil with Mrs Cawley;
others have argued that it was Addison's disease (a disorder
of the adrenal glands), tuberculosis has also been suggested,
as well as Hodgkin's disease.

Whatever it was, its unpredictability was a burden. After
a winter of sufferings, in January 1817 she could write to
niece Caroline, '*I* feel myself getting stronger than I was
half a year ago, & can so perfectly well walk to Alton, *or*
back again, without the slightest fatigue that I hope to be
able to do both when Summer comes.' And again, in the
same month she wrote to Alethea Bigg (the older sister of
Harris Bigg Wither):

> *I* have certainly gained strength through the winter and am
> not far from being well; and I think I understand my own
> case now so much better than I did, as to be able by care to
> keep off any serious return of illness. I am more & more
> convinced that *bile* is at the bottom of all I have suffered,
> which makes it easy to know how to treat myself.

You have the feeling that Jane wrote these words as much to calm her own anxieties by setting a credible version of the truth down in black and white, as to inform Alethea.

And there was still so much writing to be done. She had begun *Persuasion* in 1815, and was busy refining it into the musing, valedictory, novel it would become on publication after her death. After the magisterial performance of *Emma*, *Persuasion* seems something of a let-down – smaller, odder, sadder. It centres around the character of Anne Elliot, whose saintly patience recalls that of Fanny Price in *Mansfield Park*. The big difference is that Fanny is an ingénue, growing up before our eyes, while Anne is already twenty-seven, the age at which Jane herself closed the door on Harris Bigg Wither, the age at which one's chances of marriage start to vanish forever, 'The years of danger', the age of eternal spinsterhood.

To make things worse, Anne has once been 'An extremely pretty girl, with gentleness, modesty, taste and feeling,' but is now faded, victim of 'An early loss of bloom and spirits'. Why? Because of her great, doomed, love affair with the young naval officer Wentworth: embarked upon at the age of nineteen, when Wentworth is young, ardent, full of 'Sanguine temper and fearlessness of mind' and hopelessly poor. So poor and apparently in want of prospects, that Anne's Godmother, Lady Russell, persuades her out of the match and into what turns out to be eight years of patient self-denial. Without any prospects, and in the shadow of her sister Elizabeth, she has no choice but to trail around after her fatuous and improvident father, Sir Walter Elliot, a man who, 'For his own amusement, never took up any book but the Baronetage', and then only to review the history of his own family. It is a dreary position from which to start, and is only made worse by the reappearance of the same Wentworth, now a Captain with a fortune of £25,000 amassed in the course of a startlingly profitable career. This being Jane Austen, fidelity and propriety win through in the approved manner. But if the end is predictable enough, the hard part is reading *Persuasion* without seeing Jane herself refracted through it.

Anne Elliot has lost her looks, her vitality and her happiness at the start of the book, but by the end, has magically regained them, like a character in a fable. One thinks of Jane, the spinster aunt in the last stages of her illness, 'Languid & dull', when suffering, grateful once in awhile to recover her looks 'A little, which have been bad enough, black & white & every wrong colour. I must not depend upon being ever very blooming again' – and one thinks of *Persuasion*, which would be a strange little book to come across if one had never read any other Austen, as a piece of wish-fulfillment, a present from Jane to herself: 'It is something for a woman to be assured, in her eight-and-twentieth year, that she has not lost one charm of earlier youth.'

Even the final coming together of the happy couple (Anne and Captain Wentworth) in *Persuasion* feels more spacious and indulgent than in earlier books. Sometimes, the tone in which Jane finally pairs off Elizabeth Bennet and Mr Darcy, or Elinor Dashwood and Edward Ferrars, can seem perfunctory. But with Anne and Wentworth, she gratifies herself, imagining the triumph of love more vividly. 'You pierce my soul,' Wentworth writes to Anne;

'A word, a look will be enough to decide whether I enter your father's house this evening, or never.' Anne has a moment in which 'Her heart prophesied some mischance to damp the perfection of her felicity.' But all is well, and the couple are not only united, but are given time to themselves to reflect on what has passed, in a properly adult way. 'Would you, in short, have renewed the engagement then?' puzzles Wentworth, picking over their shared history; '"Would I!" was all her answer; but the accent was decisive enough.' What would once have been wrapped up in half a page, now sprawls over eight – Jane's last real opportunity for romance.

Apart, of course, from *Northanger Abbey*, the ghost of *Susan*, which publishers Crosby & Co. had been sitting on since the start of the century. Henry Austen, in another of his great brotherly gestures, bought the manuscript back from Crosby for the stingy £10 that they had originally paid, and then told them that it was written by the author of *Pride and Prejudice*.

Back in Jane's hands at some point in 1816, it was given a brisk working-over, which included changing the book's title, changing the main character's name and attaching a prefatory note 'By the Authoress', to account for the sometimes dated references which the book contained. Pointing out that 'This little work was finished in the year 1803,' she said, as beguilingly as she could, 'The public are entreated to bear in mind that thirteen years have passed since it was finished, many more since it was begun, and that during that period, places, manners, books, and opinions have undergone considerable changes.'

Plainly, *Northanger Abbey* lacks the coolness of mature Austen ('Is there a Henry in the world who could be insensible to such a declaration?'), and at least a third of the book is a determined, only partly entertaining, mockery of the once-popular gothic novel ('Her fearful curiosity was every moment growing greater; and seizing, with trembling hands, the hasp of the lock . . .'). With the passing years, the book has quite often come to be casually defined as a parody of a gothic novel – when it's really a playful comedy of manners, with only mildly sinister overtones, a staged bad guy in the form of General Tilney and a come-hither title. But she scrubbed it up, got on with *Persuasion* and, at the start of 1817, began work on *Sanditon*, the book she would never finish.

Cassandra had now given up her round of visits and was permanently at Chawton, looking after her sister. 'Aunt Cassandra nursed me so beautifully!' Jane wrote to Fanny Knight, not long after she was 'Almost entirely cured of my rheumatism'. Although increasingly exhausted, immobile and wearied by the presence of small children, she had plans to get out and about, in time for the spring of 1817: 'I mean to take to riding the Donkey.' The donkeys – underemployed in the winter and 'Having so long a run of luxurious idleness that I suppose we shall find they have forgotten much of their education when we use them again' – generally pulled a little two-seat open carriage. But with some coercion, a donkey could be used as one's personal mount. 'It will be more independent', Jane went on, '& less troublesome than the use of the carriage, & I shall be able to go about with At [Aunt] Cassandra in her walks to Alton and Wyards.' Which she did, going up 'Mounters Lane, &

round by where the new Cottages are to be, & found the exercise & everything very pleasant, and I had the advantage of agreeable companions, as At Cass: and Edward walked by my side. – At Cass. is such an excellent Nurse, so assiduous & unwearied!' To Caroline, she announced, 'I have taken one ride on the Donkey & like it very much – & you must try to get me quiet, mild days, that I may be able to go out pretty constantly. – A great deal of Wind does not suit me, as I have still a tendency to Rheumatism. In short I am a poor Honey at present.'

Jane had always been solicitous with regard to the health of family and friends, but now her letters were even more busy with concern for the ailing – an invalid's enthusiasm. Uncle Charles has improved 'Both as to Health, Spirits & Appearance'; but then 'Has been suffering from Rheumatism, & now he has a great eruption in his face & neck'; Jane is 'Sorry to hear of Caroline Wiggetts being so ill'; 'Mrs Wm Hammond is growing old by confinements & nursing'; nephew William 'Was bilious the other day, and Aunt Cass: supplied him with a Dose at his own request'; 'Little Harriet's headaches are abated'; 'It is impossible to be surprised at Miss Palmer's being ill'; and so on. She was moved upstairs as her illness advanced, but described herself as 'Coddled'. Her hands sometimes trembled so much that she found it difficult to write with a quill pen; so she took to a pencil on bad days. Rich Uncle Leigh Perrot died, leaving a will as generous to tiresome Aunt Perrot as it was mean-minded to the Austens. In response, Jane drafted her will at the end of April 1817. In it, she left most of her small estate to Cassandra, but with a specific legacy of £50 to Henry, who had been through illness, bankruptcy and humiliation, but who had always done what he could for her. In her life, she had earned not quite £670.

By now, she was very ill. Her 'Sad complaint' attacked her with renewed energy – 'The most severe I ever had' – but having been bedridden for days, she wrote to her friend, Anne Sharp, that '*Now*, I am getting well again, & indeed have been gradually tho' slowly recovering my strength for the last three weeks. I can sit up in my bed & employ myself, as I am proving to you at this present moment, & *really* am equal to being out of bed.' She was moved from Chawton to a house in College Street, Winchester, where the medical care would be prompter and, possibly, better.

She rallied as she told brother Edward: 'I am gaining strength very fast. I am *now* out of bed from 9 in the morng to 10 at night – upon the sopha t'is true – but I eat my meals with Aunt Cass: in a rational way, & can employ myself, and walk from one room to another.' Her bright stoicism and refusal to be dull remain; but the letters are shorter, now, and one to Edward concludes on a note of tender finality: 'If ever you are ill, may you be as tenderly nursed as I have been, may the same Blessed alleviations of anxious, simpathising friends be yours., & may you possess – as I dare say you will – the greatest blessing of all, in the consciousness of not being unworthy of their Love.' Her vigour rose and fell. Having written to Edward, she went out in a sedan-chair, and was looking forward to being promoted to a wheel-chair, if the weather held.

But July saw her final relapse. According to Cassandra, on 15 July, 'Her looks altered & she fell away;' and she was then 'hopeless of a recovery.' There was nothing to do but wait. Mary Lloyd came to help poor Cassandra – who had been almost alone in her task, for days, with only a single maidservant for assistance. Jane came to herself, briefly, on the 17th, but it was the last time. Cassandra nursed her in her last hours, a pillow in her lap to support her sister's head. When she asked Jane if she wanted anything, she answered, 'Nothing but death.' She was given something, laudanum perhaps, to ease her pain.

At last, she died in her sister's arms, at dawn on 18 July 1817. She was forty-one years old.

Cassandra was heartbroken, and wrote to Fanny Knight the saddest and most touching of letters. She said that Jane was 'The sun of my life, the gilder of every pleasure, the soother of every sorrow, I had not a thought concealed from her, & it was as if I had lost a part of myself.' Reproaching herself, she went on, 'I loved her only too well, not better than she deserved, but I am conscious that my affection for her made me sometimes unjust to & negligent of others.' And then she recounted the last hours of Jane's life, the fact that 'I was able to close her eyes myself & it was a great gratification to me to render her these last services.'

'The last sad ceremony,' the burial, remained. Women did not attend funerals in 1817. Jane was interred in Winchester Cathedral on the morning of 24 July. Her brothers Edward, Henry and Frank attended. In her next letter to Fanny, Cassandra explained how she stayed in the house, watching 'The little mournful procession the length of the street; and when it turned from my sight, and I had lost her for ever, even then I was not overpowered, nor so much agitated as I am now in writing of it.'

Jane was gone. Cassandra would live to be seventy-two: quiet, white-haired, modest and uncomplaining. The nephews and nieces would grow up. Henry saw to it that *Persuasion* and *Northanger Abbey* were published together, in December 1817. They sold tolerably well, and then Jane's books went out of print. The inscription on her tomb made no mention of her writing. Except in the memories of her family, she disappeared from view; before beginning her comeback midway through the nineteenth century. Her novels were reissued. A new audience came to appreciate her subtlety and genius. Her surviving relatives were prevailed upon to reminiscence about clever Aunt Jane.

And visitors came to Winchester Cathedral to pay their respects at the memorial stone on the floor. Eventually, the uncomprehending verger, asked so many times for directions to Jane's resting-place, was forced to enquire of yet another literary pilgrim, 'Can you tell me if there was something special about that lady?' What could one have said? That it was the books that made the lady special? Or that she would have been special if she had never written a word?

2

JANE AUSTEN – THE NOVELS

Sense and Sensibility

If *Pride and Prejudice* is Jane Austen's best-liked novel, and the one which most new readers will turn to first, *Sense and Sensibility* is quite likely to be the next one they try. Both, after all, are comedic romances; both show off Miss Austen's clever prose; their titles employ the same kind of memorable antithesis. But few readers, however much they might enjoy *Sense and Sensibility*, would rate it as highly as *Pride and Prejudice*. Why not?

Sense and Sensibility was the first of Jane Austen's novels to make it into print, in 1811, after a long process of composition, retirement and then reinvention. Jane was about twenty when she first started work on it. Called *Elinor and Marianne*, this epistolary novel acquired the title *Sense and Sensibility* a couple of years later, when she decided to give it a complete overhaul, retaining the characters of the two sisters but changing much else.

It then sat around for a decade before being taken out again, being re-worked a final time and then presented to the world as the product of two Jane Austens – the relatively blithe twenty-year-old and the wiser, shrewder, writer in her mid-thirties. When it was published, its freshness and realism won over the *Critical Review*; while the *British Critic* admired not only its deft characterizations, but also the 'Many sober and salutary maxims for the conduct of life', which women readers might extract from the novel. Lady Bessborough liked it; Princess Charlotte reckoned it 'Interesting'. And it established Austen as a writer.

After that, though, its reputation started to suffer. The keen-eyed Mrs Oliphant, one of the more important Victorian critics, observed that 'There is nothing in it that can approach within a hundred miles of the perfection of Mr Collins' – of *Pride and Prejudice* fame. Writer and critic Reginald Farrer decided in 1917 that *Sense and Sensibility* had 'The almost inevitable frigidity of a reconstruction, besides an equally inevitable uncertainty in the author's use of her weapons'. And William Empson, in the 1930s, was forced to concede that it was 'A pretty full-blown piece of romanticism, more unlike her later books than critics allow.'

For all its incidental pleasures, in other words, *Sense and Sensibility* has the unmistakable feeling of an apprentice work, of Jane Austen finding her voice and delineating her world. The result is an inconsistency of tone that one doesn't normally associate with the writer of *Emma* and

Mansfield Park. The Regency audience responded to Austen's apparent naturalism, her capacity to draw from life. Modern readers are more likely to take the realisms for granted and stub their toes on the bits that are either too blatantly structural, or too obviously hangovers from earlier fiction.

That said, she does get off to a terrific start, establishing the note of flinty candour that would inform her novels from then on as well as displaying a complete lack of squeamishness on the subject of money. The Dashwood daughters, and their mother, are poor; Mr John Dashwood, half-brother to the three girls, Elinor, Marianne and Margaret, has, thanks to the privileged status of the male offspring, inherited the family fortune, with an injunction to see that a reasonable part of it gets distributed among the women. But his ghastly wife, Mrs John Dashwood, barks him down from a gift of 'A thousand pound a-piece' to each of the girls ('enough to make them completely easy'), to 'A present of fifty pounds, now and then'. Which means, in practice, nothing – even though it allows her to conclude, with ferocious complacency, that the poor Dashwood women 'Will be much more able to give *you* something'.

The girls, sidelined from their rightful inheritance, are thus left dependent on whatever help might come their way. Austen was, by the early 1800s, well-acquainted with the anxieties of looming homelessness and genteel penury, so the sense of grievance that underpins their situation is real enough. As is the tiresome benevolence of their saviour, Sir John Middleton, his wife Lady Middleton, and his partner in mirth, Mrs Jennings. Are their garrulity and constant need for society an expression of simple high spirits, or the selfishness of the underemployed and well-to-do? Marianne sings 'Very well' for their entertainment – what choice does she have? – in response to which 'Sir John was loud in his admiration at the end of every song, and as loud in his conversation with the others while every song lasted.' The Middletons and Mrs Jennings are materially generous and unaffectedly social; they are also emotionally tone-deaf, even crass. Their charity comes at a price.

Then love enters, taking the girls' already uncertain existence and rendering it more uncertain. Everything about the romance between Marianne and Willoughby is right, and at the same time, hopelessly wrong. Marianne, the embodiment of *sensibility*, is helpless in the face of her own feelings and welcomes any yielding to emotion. She is clearly adorable – 'Her face was so lovely, that when in the common cant of praise she was called a beautiful girl, truth was less violently outraged than usually happens', as Austen puts it, both loving and broadly sarcastic – at the same time as she is fatally self-indulgent. For Marianne, if something is worth stating, it is worth overstating. 'Oh! Happy house,' she cries, on leaving Norland, the family home, 'could you know what I suffer in now viewing you from this spot, from whence perhaps I may view you no more!' And when she falls for Willoughby, she comes to the eminently passionate realization that 'Seven years would be insufficient to make some people acquainted with each other, and seven days are more than enough for others.' She is all responsiveness and worryingly unable to exert any control over the emotional messages that flash through her.

Willoughby, by the same token, is a mixture of the delightful and the unnerving. He is full of 'Manly beauty and more than common gracefulness,' a practised charmer, 'Exactly formed to engage Marianne's heart,' possessing 'Not only a captivating person, but a natural ardour of mind which was now roused and increased by the example of her own.' But alarm bells ring when he starts to poke fun at the worthy Colonel Brandon ('Who has every body's good word and nobody's notice') before taking Marianne off for a semi-licit ride in his curricle carriage, followed by a cosy inspection of Allenham, the grand estate he hopes to inherit.

We have by now adjusted to Austen's expectations of decorum, either voiced by the more staid characters (Elinor, Colonel Brandon) or expressed in the critically heightened – and *just* discordant – tone of Willoughby's banter. But deeds speak louder than words; and when sister Margaret sees Willoughby cut a lock of hair from Marianne's head, we know that a mark has been overstepped. Not long after that, Willoughby mysteriously disappears to London, 'After only ten minutes notice' and with a 'Faint smile', leaving Marianne in such a state that 'She was awake the whole night, and she wept the greatest part of it.' And we guess that Marianne's sensibility will soon enough find itself in debt to Elinor's (or possibly Colonel Brandon's) sense, if she is to survive the novel.

At this point it's customary for critics to fret over the radicalism, or otherwise, of the two sisters, Elinor and Marianne. We know that the moral direction of the novel is – broadly – conservative, with its 'Many sober and salutary maxims for the conduct of life', and Miss Austen's various authorial nudges and hints. It's possible, however, to view Marianne, with her wilfulness, her insistence on the primacy of her feelings and her centrality as an individual, as a delicious revolutionary, an embodiment of Mary Wollstonecraft's emancipated woman. But *should* we read Marianne as a kind of commentary – favourable, unfavourable or just ambivalent – on the new feminism? Quite apart from the fact that we have no idea whether Jane Austen ever actually read it, Mary Wollstonecraft's *Vindication of the Rights of Woman*, published in 1792, takes a stern line against excessive sensibility and women who are 'Blown about by every momentary gust of feeling'. For Wollstonecraft, education and an accompanying seriousness of mind are the keys to the kingdom. 'Women,' she writes, 'are capable of rationality; it only appears that they are not, because men have refused to educate them and encouraged them to be frivolous.' Which would make rational, sober, Elinor a much more likely candidate for the position of Wollstonecraft adherent. Certainly, the idea of Elinor Dashwood – a proxy for Austen herself, in many ways – sharing ideologies with Mary Wollstonecraft sounds unlikely. But an argument can be made in its favour; much as an argument can be made that Elinor is every bit as 'sensible' as her younger sister – every bit as responsive to the play of emotions within herself, and a good deal more sensitive to the emotions of others. The principal difference between Marianne and Elinor being that the latter tends to mute her feelings, to deal with them, rather than shout them to the heavens.

The notion of *Sense and Sensibility* being all about cut-and-dried antitheses takes a knock at this point. It is possible to discover ambiguities – or at least, contrary readings. But are these grey areas intended? Can they be said to contribute to the overall success of the novel? Do they suggest that Miss Austen was having some trouble in composing her characters? Was she obliged to use two heroines because that was how she had decided to shape the novel, or would one character, with a full range of ambivalences and contradictions have been better? Or is the question instead indicative of the fact that some readers have to search for hidden abstractions in order to keep themselves properly busy?

Because – to return to the story – when Willoughby departs, so does much, if not all, of the action. We are barely at the end of Volume I, and all we have to look forward to are Elinor Dashwood, who, for all her sense, her clarity and judiciousness, cannot beguile in the way her sister does; Colonel Brandon, with his 'Slight rheumatic feel in one of his shoulders' and his flannel waistcoat; and Edward Ferrars who is 'Not handsome' and whose 'Manners required intimacy to make them pleasing'. We know that *Sense and Sensibility* will turn out to be a cross between a romantic comedy and a moral fable, in which lessons will be learned and virtue rewarded. But we do need a sense of purpose, or, failing that, some entertainment, on the way. Austen's heroines are bound by the rules of propriety, restricting free movement and initiative, so we cannot normally look to them for sudden plot twists. But the story must be made to move forward somehow, or even the most loyal reader will start hunting for subtexts.

And so it is that the plot moves us to London with Mrs Jennings, where Marianne's efforts to make contact with

Willoughby are at first rebuffed, before being absolutely flattened when he reveals (by letter, like a coward) that 'My affections have been long engaged elsewhere, and it will not be many weeks, I believe, before this engagement is fulfilled'. The relationship is conclusively over by the book's halfway point, and something else must be found to take its place. Now, this abandonment of the Willoughby–Marianne affair may be structurally necessary, laying the foundations for all the thematic entanglements and resolutions to come; but it is also typical of Austen to be so concerned with her didactic purpose that she squares away storylines before we have really finished with them.

So we look to the secondary characters for interest – and luckily find it in the form of the pleasingly monstrous Lucy Steele, 'Ignorant and illiterate', deficient 'Of all mental improvement', endowed with 'Little sharp eyes', and engaged to be married to Elinor's object of interest, Edward Ferrars.

One wonders how earlier generations of Austen readers could have doted so sentimentally on innocent, homely, 'Dear Jane' and her 'Dear Books': Lucy Steele is a bracingly sour invention, the product of a literary imagination that can readily express malice and vanity, and, in consequence, generate one of the best episodes in the novel. Spread across two chapters, Miss Steele's long and shameless account of her four-year secret engagement, the apparently limitless wait for Mrs Ferrars to die and leave her money to Edward, and his desire to take the cloth are described. Best of all, Chapter Twenty-Two reveals Lucy's desire for Elinor to give her wise advice as to what to do next. Elinor writhes and we writhe with her, as Lucy prattles on ('Amiably bashful, with only one side glance at her companion to observe its effect on her') infinitely conscious that Elinor is more interested in Edward than she lets on: 'If you could be supposed to be biassed in any respect by your own feelings,' she observes, 'your opinion would not be worth having.' This is our reward. When we encounter Lucy Steele, we see Jane Austen's talent as a writer burgeoning in front of us – in her ability to fix a character who is not just scandalizing, but also credible.

The character of Lucy Steele is used structurally, too. One of *Sense and Sensibility*'s presiding themes concerns precedence – between men and women (sons who inherit and daughters who don't); between older and younger siblings (Elinor and Marianne; Edward and Robert Ferrars); between first and second romantic attachments (where even Colonel Brandon has had a prior love, the 'first' Eliza). In this respect, Lucy helps fill out the rather Augustan symmetries of the story. But she also points to a grim reality: one must be provided for; one must marry. After all, why would the idiotic Mrs Palmer put up with surly Mr Palmer ('What do you think he said when he heard of your coming with mama? I forget what it was now, but it was something so droll!') if not because, thanks to marriage to Mr Palmer, she has material comfort and is not a spinster. The need to secure money, and the dread of being left on the shelf – money and marriage – the *desiderata* of Austen's world, weigh on Lucy Steele's mind as much as they must on Elinor and Marianne's.

Only now, Elinor and Marianne are becalmed, yet again. Another lurch forward in the plot: this time courtesy of Colonel Brandon, who appears unexpectedly at the door.

It is, of course, Willoughby who is the reason for Brandon's visit. Marianne takes herself off to her room, while Elinor is given the full story, alone. And what a story it is. It seems to come, in fact, from a different novel altogether, from an earlier kind of fiction, from a Richardson or a Fanny Burney: the terrible ill-treatment of Eliza by Brandon's own brother, her divorce and fall, her death by consumption and then worse – the revelation that Eliza has given birth to an illegitimate daughter, Little Eliza, over whom Brandon has assumed a tender guardianship, followed by the bombshell that this young woman has been seduced by 'Expensive, dissipated' Willoughby and left with child. It thus turns out that Brandon has been materially involved in two personal catastrophes, the second a variation on the first, and has even fought a duel with Willoughby in an attempt to settle the score. As Elinor puts it, 'This is beyond everything!' Beyond everything, and not in the best interests of the novel, for at least two reasons.

First, the Willoughby backstory, although potentially full of dramatic energy, is more a distraction than a dynamic force: it may add to our detestation of Willoughby, but there's nothing much Austen can do with it. Framed by Colonel Brandon's judicious narrative, it becomes a piece of inert material, however scandalous.

Secondly, it brings Colonel Brandon to the fore again. Although his interest in Marianne has been signalled from the start, our natural inclination is to see this as a feint on Austen's part, with Brandon as a more natural partner for Elinor. But however decent he is, however much he chimes in with Elinor's view of the world, however much he appears and re-appears in the story – fixing up Edward

Ferrars here, revealing the truth about Willoughby there – he never quite comes to life. Instead he exists as a kind of superhuman butler, indeterminately aged somewhere between Elinor's generation and her mother's, arranging things behind the scenes and ultimately ensuring a satisfactory outcome. Indeed, faced with the choice of reading about him and, say, Lucy Steele, the average reader would opt for Lucy and all her entertaining beastliness, rather than worthy Brandon – a surely unintended consequence, but one with implications for the rest of the story.

What happens next is an increasingly uneven mixture of social comedy and morally themed plot-fixing. The Willoughby story has invaded the mood of the book: Marianne has sunk into a depression, indifferent 'To her dress and appearance'; Edward Ferrars has very properly refused to ditch Lucy Steele in order to placate his mother; and even Mrs Jennings has acquired a new note of moral depth. Not only does she recount the public discovery of the Lucy Steele engagement, she brings to it a sense of correctness which redefines her, persuading us that there is more to her than just tactlessness and a big voice ('He has acted like an honest man!' she pronounces). To wrap it all up, Colonel Brandon rewards Edward Ferrars for his moral tenacity by offering him the living at Delaford Parsonage.

It is a lot to get through, and even though it provides an excuse for more sharp mockery of John Dashwood and Robert Ferrars, as well as a chance for Marianne to achieve a new and essential recognition of her own place in the moral scheme of things ('Oh! Elinor,' she cries, on learning of Elinor's patient stoicism in the face of Lucy Steele, 'you have made me hate myself for ever'), the very fact that there

is such a clear division of labour between the comedy and
the moral message hints at the difficulties Austen is having
in combining all the elements of her story. In fact, the tone
takes a final turn from high moral drama to melodrama
once the girls and Mrs Jennings have been relocated to
Cleveland, the Palmers' Somerset house. This, it turns out,
is only eighty miles from Barton Cottage, and a mere thirty
from Combe Magna, Willoughby's old home. Marianne is
vulnerable again. The moment she sets foot in Cleveland,
her heart begins 'Swelling with emotion' at the proximity
of so many memories; so she decides to deal with her inner
torment by taking as many long, solitary walks as possible.

She heads for the remotest, most overgrown places,
'Where there was something more of wildness than in the
rest', where the Revd William Gilpin and The Picturesque
might be found, and where everything is soaking wet with
rain. She catches a cold, which turns into a fever with,
worse still, 'A putrid tendency.' Given that Jane and
Cassandra Austen had both very nearly died from the
'Putrid fever' in childhood, this is clearly no small matter.
The Romantic melancholy that led Marianne to take her
solitary walks, turns out to be the thing that now threatens
her life. She grows 'More heavy, restless and uncomfortable', fails to respond to the interventions of Mr Harris, the
apothecary, and becomes delirious, until at last, 'With
feverish wildness', she cries out 'Is mamma coming?'

Sense and Sensibility is a novel full of ineffectual or
indifferent mothers, but Mrs Dashwood, who has returned
home to Barton, must nevertheless be summoned by
Colonel Brandon. Marianne sinks lower, 'In an heavy
stupor', while Elinor and Mrs Jennings foresee the 'Early

death of a girl so young, so lovely as Marianne'. And then she rallies. Mr Harris confirms that the recovery has begun. Mrs Jennings retires to sleep. 'The night,' we are told, 'was cold and stormy. The wind roared round the house, and the rain beat against the windows.' A carriage drives up to the house, its lamps flaring. Elinor hurries down the stairs, rushes into the drawing-room ... 'And saw only Willoughby'.

Thus commences a showdown between the two moral forces of the novel. *The* showdown, in fact, and another take on *Sense and Sensibility* – with 'sensibility' now represented by Willoughby, soul-mate to Marianne and just as helplessly prey to his own emotions. The wind howls outside, Mrs Jennings has passed out in her bedroom, and there is Elinor, alone with Mr Willoughby, a creature of scarcely plausible villainy. We are a long way from the barbed comedy of Mr and Mrs Palmer, Lucy Steele, Mrs Ferrars and Robert Ferrars. But what do we make of it?

For a start, we begin to suspect that Marianne's illness has become not much more than a literary contrivance to get Willoughby to confront his own nature. But when Willoughby says 'I felt that she was infinitely dearer to me than any other woman in the world', we suspect that this has already been achieved by what has passed between the two lovers. At the same time, Willoughby seems ready enough to dismiss his ill-treatment of poor Eliza with a mere 'I heartily wish it had never been'. So to what extent has he arrived at a true assessment of himself? Elinor, too, seems reluctant to come to a judgement, finding first that Willoughby's words 'In spite of herself made her think him sincere', before turning on him 'With the most angry contempt,' then feeling 'A little softened' and *then* 'Hardening her heart anew against any compassion for him'.

In the end, nothing about Willoughby is calculated to make us feel any warmer towards him. Having been disinherited by his wealthy relation, Mrs Smith, he is thrown a lifeline by that same woman – marry the wronged Eliza, and the money will be his again – only to reject it out of hand ('That could not be'). Instead, he goes ahead and makes his advantageous connection with Miss Grey and her fifty thousand pounds, submitting to her jealous wrath and allowing her to dictate his final letter to Marianne, 'Servilely copying such sentences as I was ashamed to put my name to.' This is a moment which reveals Jane Austen as the tyro novelist, caught somewhere between the conventions of existing literary forms and her own ambitions.

Still, at least two verities emerge from it. If Willoughby's morals seem unimproved, he – and we – do learn this: that love, real, sincere love, is an overmastering force, so overmastering that it compels even *him* to chase through the night in order to beg for some kind of reconciliation. The climactic Willoughby–Elinor scene doesn't read much like Jane Austen, and can even be criticized as a betrayal of the bright promise of the first third of the novel. But it does contain a truth central to her writing, and one that will inform it for the rest of her career – that love, indeed, conquers all. And then on the final page, it affords us a glimpse of the cool worldliness that is Austen's trademark. Willoughby 'Lived to exert, and frequently to enjoy himself. His wife was not always out of humour, nor his home always uncomfortable; and in his breed of horses and dogs, and in sporting of every kind, he found no inconsiderable degree of felicity.' In other words, Willoughby does not suffer the rest of his days in well-heeled misery, as seemed likely a few chapters earlier. It is the sort of truth that Austen, among all the final convenient marriages (including the Dashwood family's leaning on Marianne in a faintly sinister 'confederacy' to attach herself to the old Colonel), is so good at.

And it becomes a final justification for *Sense and Sensibility*. The realization of its promise comes in the next book, and the ones after that. Perhaps the best thing about *Sense and Sensibility* is that it is the first term in the series, and its flaws are all permissible because they can be redeemed.

Pride and Prejudice

With *Pride and Prejudice* we leave the world of mere novel-writing, and enter the world of popularity contests. *Pride and Prejudice* is not just many Austen-lovers' favourite work, it is routinely voted one of the most popular novels of all time, by any writer. It has been turned into movies, TV series, musicals and stage plays. It was clearly a favourite of Jane herself, who called it 'My own darling child', and expressed a candid partiality for the character of Elizabeth Bennet. It has not only given us the imperishable Mr Darcy – by now, a shorthand for any lowering, hard-to-get fictional male love interest – it has given us Mr Collins, Mr Bennet, Lady Catherine de Bourgh, one of the most famous opening lines in English literature, and an all-purpose template for romantic fiction. It is, in fact, something of a prodigy.

It's not hard to see why it should be so popular. Quite apart from its blithe first half and the humbling of the arrogant hero it depicts in the second, it has taken many of the best elements of *Sense and Sensibility* – playful satire, love intrigues, sharp dialogue – and refined them into a tighter, more efficient whole. It features Elizabeth Bennet as an appealingly active, rather than wearyingly submissive, heroine. It is nowhere near as didactic in tone as *Sense and Sensibility*, even going as far as to gently mock Dr James Fordyce's *Sermons to Young Women* of 1766, a collection of instructive homilies intended to fortify modesty and virtue. It is still ideologically conservative – but relaxed enough to give a very fair hearing to Sir William Lucas, who has made his money through trade, rather than inheritance or advantageous marriage; and critical enough of Lady Catherine de Bourgh, who, despite being a member of the minor nobility, is guilty of 'Ill breeding'. It even inhabits a morally ambiguous world, in which the central characters are allowed to behave well *and* badly; in which unworthy compromise (Charlotte and Mr Collins) is admitted as a fact of life; in which parents (Mr and Mrs Bennet) are feckless and selfish, but nonetheless parents; and in which mildly vicious folly (Lydia and Wickham) goes pretty much unpunished. It is a suspiciously modern-looking landscape, at the same time as it enjoys all the benefits of Austen's quiet take on the Regency period; and it requires very little effort to feel at home there.

This malleability extends to the two star players. Although the title, *Pride and Prejudice*, echoes the anti-thetical form of *Sense and Sensibility*, the distinctions between the two protagonists are not clear-cut. We know that Darcy is proud, not least because people keep saying he is ('He was the proudest, most disagreeable man in the world'; 'His pride, his abominable pride'; 'That tall, proud man'). And we know that Elizabeth is prejudiced, not least because *she* says she is ('Blind, partial, prejudiced, absurd'). But pride and prejudice are related concepts, two aspects of the same predisposition; just as Elizabeth and Darcy jointly exist in a way distinct from the other characters – both are glamorous and haughty, his aristocratic disdain sanctioned by wealth and family connections and hers by the natural aristocracy of beauty and wit. 'I could easily forgive *his* pride,' as Elizabeth puts it, 'if he had not mortified *mine*.' And both, by the same token, are obliged to undergo that painful process of self-understanding which is at the heart of Austen's novels, and without which no ending can properly be delivered.

So. The Bennets are a noisy, rackety family of five daughters – Jane, Elizabeth, Lydia, Kitty and Mary – headed by the more-or-less delinquent Mr Bennet and the garrulous Mrs Bennet. Mr Bennet is a father who has abdicated many of the responsibilities of parenthood in favour of a posture of more or less continuous mockery of the human condition. The good news is that his apparent laxity has – in a faint echo of life in the Austen household – allowed his girls to read as much as they like, and civilize themselves accordingly. 'Such of us as wished to learn, never wanted the means', Elizabeth explains to a frankly scornful Lady de Bourgh. 'We were always encouraged to read, and had all the masters that were necessary.' Two of the daughters are, however, largely superfluous to the plot: Kitty and Mary (Austen hasn't yet acquired the sheer narrative concentration she would display in *Emma*). As well as slightly too many daughters, there's something of an overlap between self-effacing older sister Jane and Elizabeth's confidante, Charlotte Lucas, with her modesty and quiet wisdoms ('There are very few of us who have heart enough to be really in love without encouragement').

But Austen's powers as a writer are advancing, and she manages to find room in the crowd for the bewitching Elizabeth. Elizabeth combines a thoroughly progressive independence of mind with a dangerously Marianne Dashwood degree of spontaneity. It's worth noting that if Elinor Dashwood was one kind of stand-in for Jane Austen, then Elizabeth, with her literary tastes, zesty intelligence, lustrous eyes, slim figure and love of dancing, does seem awfully close to being a tastefully fictionalized version of the other, more fun-filled Jane. And *this* Jane is allowed to provoke Mr Darcy for chapter after chapter: meeting him hauteur for hauteur; turning what would have been a hopeless lapse of decorum – arriving at the Bingley house, muddied, 'Her hair so untidy, so blowsy!', her face 'Glowing with the warmth of exercise', having tramped three miles across country in order to make sure that her ailing sister was being cared for – into another seduction; leaving Darcy unable to do anything but sigh over how her beautiful eyes 'Were brightened by the exercise'. This, unlike Marianne Dashwood's near-fatal walk in the rain, calls down no punishment – the reverse, in fact, with Darcy, fully 'agitated', blurting out at the halfway point that 'My feelings will not be repressed. You must allow me to tell you how ardently I admire and love you.'

It is a terrific performance, completely beguiling, sexy –

and yet without any real impropriety. Austen goes out of her way to make it clear that Elizabeth is incontrovertibly *not* setting her cap at Darcy, despite the constant background noise of marriage plans involving Bingley, Collins and the chorus of daughters. And despite the infamous tease of the opening line: the 'Truth universally acknowledged, that a single man in possession of a good fortune, must be in want of a wife.' The fundamental needs of Austen's world – money and marriage – are as pressing as ever, but they don't have quite the same deadly urgency as they did in *Sense and Sensibility*, nor the same capacity to get between the reader and the main characters, and sour the tone of the whole novel. Certainly, the Bennet family is under a financial cloud, in the form of the entail which gifts the family fortune, such as it is, to Mr Collins. But this is a lot less disruptive than being turned out of one's own home and left to the charity of others, as happens to the Crawfords. And it's part of the confident charm of *Pride and Prejudice* that Austen takes that problem – Mr Collins – and has such fun with him. She is also confident enough to introduce Mr Bingley – 'Good looking and gentlemanlike', with his estate of 'Nearly an hundred thousand pounds' – at the start of the novel, only to reveal this as a diversion when we discover that the real story centres on Darcy and Elizabeth. And then, having assembled her cast and her *mise-en-scène*, Austen is relaxed enough to give them the time and space they need to fully develop.

After all, not much happens for the first third of the book, except for visits, meals, chance encounters, domestic entertainments and some dancing: the natural material of Jane Austen's own world. References to the militia, and by extension, the interminable war with post-Revolutionary France, certainly locate the action in time, but carry a very quiet political message. And the vexed question of the Regency might as well not exist. And yet, of course, so much happens in the texture of the language, and the evolving relationships it describes. You can find incident in anything from Austen's elegant, pointed, throwaways (such as the one directed at the stuffy Mary Bennet – ' "Pride," observed Mary, who piqued herself upon the solidity of her reflections, "is a very common failing I believe" '), to Elizabeth's glitteringly epigrammatic rebuke, directed at Darcy ('We are each of an unsocial, taciturn disposition, unwilling to speak, unless we expect to say something that will amaze the whole room, and be handed down to posterity with all the eclat of a proverb.'). There is a fount of delight in Mr Collins, going his own fatuous way, unperturbed when faced with the notion that Elizabeth may not want to marry him ('As I must therefore conclude that you are not serious in your rejection of me, I shall chuse to attribute it to your wish of increasing my love by suspense, according to the usual practice of elegant fe- males.'). There is Mr Bennet, gloating over Mr Collins' 'Servility and self-importance.' And there is Mr Wickham. Wickham looks like another Willoughby: 'He had all the best part of beauty, a fine countenance, a good figure, and very pleasing address.' Bingley is good-looking, too; and Darcy has 'Handsome features' and a 'Noble mien'. But Wickham has none of Bingley's modesty, nor Darcy's grandeur. Instead, he is 'Completely charming', a formula- tion which will turn out to be every bit as sinister as it sounds. Charm which is *complete*, which leaves no room for marks of virtue or human quiddity, soon betrays itself; and before too long, Wickham has begun his assault on Darcy's character.

At this point, the progress of *Pride and Prejudice*, which has been so convincing, stumbles. We have been moving forwards almost seamlessly, but now we must start backtracking: first with Wickham's complaint about Darcy; then with Colonel Fitzwilliam's revelation that Darcy put a stop to the Bingley–Jane Bennet romance; then with Darcy's letter of self-justification (concerning Bingley) and rebuttal (concerning Wickham). We know that this sort of thing is important for plot complication and in order to establish false conceptions, which can then be put right in the course of the book. But it is disruptive. The linear narrative is all of a piece with the novel's naturalistic setting, its just observations and its deftly characterized dialogue. Austen's genius is inevitably seen at its best when event proceeds from character, not from back-filling. Once we start on revelations and buried histories, things get stagy; we sense the dead hand of the writer building in plot development; it starts to look like period fiction.

So the novel changes gear, and we have no choice but to go along with it. The militia – and Wickham – are leaving. Lydia Bennet has outlined her main preoccupations, calling out 'Have you seen any pleasant men? Have you had any flirting?' before disappearing off to Brighton. And Mr Bennet fears the worst: 'Lydia will never be easy till she has exposed herself in some public place or other.' Everything has been set in train, and Austen's purpose from the start of Volume III is to invoke a new kind of sobriety: 'To Pemberley, therefore, they were to go.' This ringing command is followed by Elizabeth's first sight of Pemberley House in Derbyshire – Darcy's splendid country seat and, in many ways, the source of his numinous power. This, in turn, is followed by one of *those* moments in the novel – the one where Elizabeth finally yields: 'At that moment she felt, that to be mistress of Pemberley might be something!'

Now, what do we make of this? On the one hand, it looks as if independent, clever, energetic Elizabeth Bennet is just like any other languishing spinster who goes to pieces the moment she's confronted with real wealth. On the other hand, this is Jane Austen, and a proper respect for money, although essential, has less to do with Elizabeth's intentions than do Pemberley's visible signs of taste, reticence and discrimination. The stream running through the landscaped grounds is devoid of 'Any artificial appearance. Its banks were neither formal, nor falsely adorned.' Elizabeth has never seen a place 'For which nature had done more, or where natural beauty had been so little counteracted by an awkward taste.' There is decency and a respect for the natural order, which continues once she, and her aunt and uncle, are inside the house. 'Every disposition of the ground – "viewed from the interior" – was good.' And the fixtures and fittings are in a style which is neither 'Gaudy nor uselessly fine'. Mrs Reynolds, the housekeeper, shows them around, explaining that Mr Darcy is every bit as admirable as the surroundings he inhabits: 'He is' – apparently – 'the best landlord, and the best master that ever lived.' Which is then corroborated by Darcy himself, who suddenly appears from the back of the building, no longer the haughty meddler, but full of 'civility' and 'gentleness', inviting Elizabeth's uncle to stay and enjoy the fishing. There is congruence between the landscape and its owner, a shared, unforced rightness. It is a moral landscape. And it's this, not a dream of hard cash, which sets Elizabeth off.

But then the problem is: where to go next? After all, Elizabeth has spent most of the book keeping her feelings for Darcy at arm's length. How can Austen negotiate her towards some kind of tenderness?

Some preliminary work has already been done. A turning point was reached some time before, when Elizabeth, reflecting on Darcy's letter to her, acknowledged her past errors: 'How despicably have I acted!' she lamented, brooding on her mistaken dogmatism, 'I, who have prided myself on my discernment!' And, more dramatically, she declares that 'Till this moment, I never knew myself.' Self-knowledge is a prerequisite of the well-tempered mind, along with humility and gratitude; and it is gratitude which now draws her closer to Darcy. 'There was a motive within her of good will which could not be overlooked. It was gratitude.' Moreover, Darcy's new, amiable ways, 'Excited not only astonishment but gratitude'. And in case we're in any doubt: 'She respected, she esteemed, she was grateful to him.' It is a start. But more will have to be done. Austen cannot betray Elizabeth's character, her quiddity, her underlying conservatism, by having her discover a sudden concealed passion for Darcy. Instead, the final push will have to be made by Darcy himself.

It's at this point that the Lydia–Wickham story comes into its own, along with a tonal shift not so much into the melodrama of *Sense and Sensibility*, but towards a kind of grim farce. The subterfuges and their flight to Gretna Green in Scotland could easily have turned into a rehash of Willoughby's old criminalities, with a breathless denouement and a pervasive sense of disapproval. But Austen's tolerably relaxed, worldly account of the event not only sits better with the rest of the novel, it gives Darcy room to operate without being stifled by questions of morality. Lydia's letter to her friend, Harriet Forster, can be as foolish as she likes, without veering anywhere near tragedy: 'I am going to Gretna Green, and if you cannot guess with who, I shall think you a simpleton.' Equally, it allows Mr Collins to make a superbly canting return to the action in *his* letter, in which he assures Mr Bennet that 'The death of your daughter would have been a blessing in comparison of this'; and that 'This false step in one daughter, will be injurious to the fortunes of all the others, for who, as lady Catherine herself condescendingly says, will connect themselves with such a family.' It even allows Mr Bennet, in his one moment of agony – 'No, Lizzy, let me once in my life feel how much I have been to blame' – to add a typically cynical qualification: 'I am not afraid of being overpowered by the impression. It will pass away soon enough.'

But this change in tone is more than just comic relief. It is an enabler: after all, if the elopement really is the inescapable moral tragedy Mr Collins seems to think it is, Darcy shouldn't take a hand in it; but if the narrative that frames it can make it seem somehow less than tragic, then his intervention is both welcome and necessary, in order to throw some kind of respectable covering over the affair. So, Lydia, on her return, is not just happy to be Mrs Wickham, but aggressively keen to demonstrate her happiness, taunting one of her former dalliances by letting her hand 'Just rest upon the window frame, so that he might see the ring, and then I bowed and smiled like any thing.' Mr Bennet quickly comes to terms with his son-in-law – 'He simpers, and smirks and makes love to us all. I am prodigiously proud of him.' And the dispensation even extends as far as Elizabeth, who speaks kindly to the cowed Wickham, holding out her hand to him – which he kisses 'With affectionate gallantry, though he hardly knew where to look'. It seems that we all, readers as well as characters, can have our cake and eat it. We can be morally informed, we can even forgive – but we need not go short of comic entertainment on the way.

Darcy, meanwhile, has been through such superhuman exertions – tracking down the runaways, overcoming his horror of having to deal with such wastrels, haggling with Wickham, paying off his debts and securing his commission – it's difficult to reconcile him with the starchy grandee of the first volume of the novel. Clearly, though, his work is starting to pay off. Elizabeth, on learning of the effort he has put in, is allowed to unbend towards him a little further ('Her heart did whisper, that he had done it for her'). But he has still more to do: there is the debt to Jane Bennet – his thwarting of her relationship with Bingley – that must be paid. For a while this exists as a counterpoint to Elizabeth's own feelings. As she frets over Darcy ('Teazing, teazing, man!') so she frets over Bingley ('Oh, Jane, take care'), suffering both for herself and her sister. For this she is recompensed twice. Bingley's 'ductility' comes in handy, as Darcy can steer him back towards Miss Bennet without too much trouble; while Elizabeth can at last access that virtuous affection which has been maturing throughout the second half of the story. Darcy has humbled himself more times than anyone would have believed possible, while she receives 'With gratitude and pleasure, his present assurances'.

And what do we make of the place they now inhabit? Austen has given us examples of several kinds of marriage: the marriage of utility (Charlotte and Mr Collins); a marriage of necessity (Lydia and Wickham); another based on attraction, but with a confusion of motives (Jane and Bingley); another, in its autumn years, hanging on through convention (Mr and Mrs Bennet); and, at some point in the future, the marriage between Darcy and Elizabeth. And of all these marriages, we feel confident that Darcy and Elizabeth's will be the most interesting (if not the most secure), not least because – while she may have changed her mind – Elizabeth is the only person not to have compromised. Indeed, her ebullience is as undimmed at the end of the book as it is at the beginning: 'Elizabeth's spirits soon rising to playfulness again, she wanted Mr Darcy to account for his ever having fallen in love with her.' The suffering which brings self-knowledge has almost all been experienced by others (although in Mr Collins' particularly stubborn case, with no increase in self-knowledge), allowing Elizabeth Bennet to live in a world of perfect comedy, a prelapsarian world. It would never be this simple again.

Mansfield Park

By the time *Mansfield Park* was published, in 1814, Jane Austen was a very different person from the young woman who had first drafted *Sense and Sensibility* and *Pride and*

Prejudice. She had left Steventon, endured the stay in Bath, lost her father, had – perhaps – a last, failed, attempt at romance in Sidmouth, stared privation in the face and finally been installed at Chawton on the charitable impulse of her brother. She was well into her thirties, a confirmed spinster, and life had proven itself to be more irksome and challenging than she might have pictured it in her early twenties. She was older, rather more sober, and her experiences inevitably coloured the novel she began writing in 1811.

As a result, anyone coming to *Mansfield Park* in search of another playful romantic comedy, will be disappointed. The heroine, Fanny Price, is a long way from being instantly loveable. The action is somehow minimal and dense at the same time. The morality is narrowly inflexible, with only the tiresomely worthy Fanny (if you take the majority view – the writer Jay McInerney admitted to having 'A bit of a sneaker for her') coming out with any credit. It's also a fairly long book, even if you like it. On the other hand, the satire in *Mansfield Park* is as mordant and sharply conceived as anything Miss Austen wrote. The characters are both complex and complete. And the structure – always an issue with the earlier novels – is now cunningly framed, subtle and controlled. It is, for all its difficult reputation, a mature novel, proof that Jane Austen's talents had been growing and deepening in the long interval following *Pride and Prejudice*. Why, one might ask, should it be such an effort to extract the entertainment? Why can't the book try harder to come to the reader? *Mansfield Park*, like *Emma*, which follows it, is one of those books whose surface simplicity is an act of concealment. It needs therefore to be read fairly carefully and fairly slowly; and then the cleverness becomes clear. Not everyone, however, will be prepared to stick around that long.

But first, Fanny Price. The critic Lionel Trilling remarked that 'No one, I believe, has ever found it possible to like the heroine of *Mansfield Park*'. C. S. Lewis claimed that Austen had put nothing into Fanny 'Except rectitude of mind', and that – worse – 'One of the most dangerous of literary ventures is the little, shy, unimportant heroine whom none of the other characters value. The danger is that your readers may agree with the other characters.' Kingsley Amis loathed her. Even Jane Austen's own mother found her 'insipid'. And she doesn't fit at all well into the modern world. What, exactly, is Fanny Price supposed to be?

There are clearly elements of Austen's own family experiences contained in her story – the Portsmouth background reminds us of the two Naval brothers; the gifting of Fanny to her wealthy uncle's family at the age of ten recalls Edward Austen's similar dispatch to the Knights at the age of fifteen. But the fictional tone is altogether darker. Fanny's vaguely indigent Portsmouth mother 'Could hardly have made a more untoward choice' of marriage partner; while her induction into the world of stately Mansfield Park is as fraught as Edward Austen's into Godmersham seems to have been agreeable. Painfully shy and uncertain, Fanny, 'Whether near or from her cousins, whether in the school-room, the drawing-room; or the shrubbery, was equally forlorn, finding something to fear in every person and place.' The fact of her being sent to live with her relations is not a cruelty in itself. But her enforced friendlessness, her alienation, her helplessness, her cousins' reckoning her 'Cheap on finding that she had but two sashes, and had never learnt French', her lonely white attic bedroom and her cold little sitting-room in which no fire is ever lit, clearly are.

Determinedly unyielding readers might see in this a pre-Dickensian mawkishness. Where, they might wonder, is the Marianne Dashwood, the Elizabeth Bennet, to show some passion, some independence of spirit? Fanny's misery is tempered only by sweet-natured Edmund Bertram taking pity on her and assisting her 'With his penknife or his orthography' when she writes to her brother William. And this limpness persists throughout the greater part of the book, whether Fanny is going for a walk, standing in the sun or taking part in amateur theatricals. She grows up, she becomes a woman, but she shrinks, nearly all the time, from what is new or threatening. She is sensitive to nature and Cowper's poems. She is reduced to tears by the offer of a glass of Madeira wine. Still: Austen is working out a plan, and we must stick with it for the subsequent rewards to become obvious. Arguably the best thing is to try and access one's own feelings of frailty and injustice; and recall that Miss Austen must have been doing something similar herself when she invented Fanny in the first place.

Besides, she has thrown in a couple of genuine literary monsters to keep us happy while the story consolidates. There is Lady Bertram, the essence of supine self-absorption; and the infinitely more dynamic Mrs Norris, a nightmare vision of parsimony, snobbery and opportunism. Mrs Norris' scrupulous meanness ('I really should not have a bed to give her, for I must keep a spare room for the friend') is structurally necessary, too, as it gives Fanny something to work against in the early stages of the novel, and provides a counter to any conviction we might have that Fanny's dismal vulnerability is *all* the product of her own want of character.

And then Fanny matures a bit, the young people assume centre stage, and in a way, the novel really begins. Surprisingly quickly, Fanny Price, the Bertram children, the Crawfords, Mr Rushworth and, later, Mr Yates, fill the pages. At this point, time invested in Fanny Price begins to pay off. Austen herself said, rather cryptically, that *Mansfield Park* was a novel about 'Ordination'. But whether it's wholly or only partly about Edmund Bertram's chosen career, *Mansfield Park* is also unequivocally a Bildungsroman, a dark comedy of manners, and an investigation into human frailty and, to top it off, a critique of youthful insincerity. Tom Bertram and the Bertram sisters are bad enough (Julia Bertram, gazing slyly at her sister and the leaden Mr Rushworth, says, 'Do look at Mr Rushworth and Maria, standing side by side, exactly as if the ceremony were going to be performed'), but the sexy Crawfords, fresh from London and their degenerate uncle's household, are worse – haloed as they are by selfishness from the moment they turn up in sleepy Northampton-shire. Witness Mary Crawford, vapouring over the diffi-culty of getting porterage for her harp in the depths of the country ('I found that I had been asking the most unreasonable, most impossible thing in the world, had offended all the farmers, all the labourers, all the hay in the parish'), and Henry, bent on his seduction of the older Miss Bertram ('I think it might be done, if you really wished to be more at large, and could allow yourself to think it not prohibited'). Is this Jane Austen, the middle-aged writer, looking back severely on a generation she has outgrown? Is it Jane Austen looking forward more largely, to a time of social instability and ungoverned change? Is it Jane Austen making a point about the verities of settled country life in contradistinction to the febrile novelties of city life?

The answers will have to wait. In the immediate experience of reading *Mansfield Park*, what first fixes us are questions of tone and technique. *Mansfield Park* is a novel in which plays and acting form a central theme – and in its broader construction the book can be read as a succession of almost stage-bound events. Mansfield Park being, for the most part, the formal setting; with a more-or-less unchanging cast. This narrowness of resources actually yields benefits for Miss Austen and her readers. The writing becomes (in contrast) more spacious, allowing the characters to breathe and giving Austen time to unpick their motives and their emotions. It also creates the conditions in which narrative can emerge from character, in which the latter drives the former, in a properly modern interpretation of the capabilities of the novel. No more handy flashback revelations or propitious lurches in the action; instead, we experience an apparently seamless partnership between psychology and story.

Which has implications for Fanny. By the time we reach the great walk around Mr Rushworth's grounds, in Chapter Nine, all the main characters have been introduced, and all of them – with the exception of Edmund Bertram – have turned out to be venal, affected, deluded, vain or lacking in moral sense. Dialogue illuminates character; and action (Maria Bertram and Henry Crawford escaping through the gate into the park, while Maria's sweetheart, Mr Rushworth, stumbles off to look for the key) expresses it. 'The young people were pleased with each other from the first', and now they are desperate to flirt and behave badly. Even Edmund, caught up in the tizzy of frivolity, hankers after the 'Remarkably pretty' Mary Crawford, with her 'Great cleverness as a horsewoman'.

Fanny meanwhile has to remain observant but uncommitted, a kind of human *tabula rasa* in the middle of the action, a moral presence, but principally a recorder of events. She has a difficult job. Her passivity can easily be read as feebleness; her capacity for being shocked ('Astonished at Miss Bertram, and angry with Mr Crawford') as priggishness. But she is the lens through which we watch the others incriminate themselves, and at the same time she provides a handy tonal counterpoint to the bright chatter of the pleased young people. So the scene of the walk – with the restless Mary Crawford bewitching Edmund Bertram, and Henry Crawford doing the same to Maria Bertram – revolves around a still centre: Fanny, parked on a bench in a glade. The scintillating misrule promised ever since the Crawfords' arrival, becomes a reality, and, 'Since the day at Sotherton,' Fanny 'could never see Mr Crawford with either sister without observation, and seldom without wonder or censure.'

Where, though, can Fanny go from this point? We are barely a quarter of the way through the book. What can Austen do to keep Fanny at the centre of the action? And how can she maintain Edmund Bertram's interest? Because Fanny is a Jane Austen heroine, after all, and marriage and money underpin everything just as much as they ever did; and we want to know how she is going to manage in this particular lottery. Luckily, she is not only virtuous, but, as the story progresses, increasingly attractive. We know this not least because, by the halfway mark, even Henry Crawford has woken up to this reality. 'I cannot be satisfied without Fanny Price,' he murmurs, evilly, 'without making a hole in Fanny Price's heart.' Once 'Quiet, modest, not plain looking', she has become 'Absolutely pretty. I used to think she had neither complexion nor countenance; but in that soft skin of her's, so frequently tinged with a blush as it was yesterday, there is decided beauty.' Austen's Cinderella is acquiring powers that one could not have anticipated at the start.

But the young gadabouts are now planning something more unsettling than a stroll in the park. With Sir Thomas Bertram long gone to inspect his possessions in Antigua (causing some critics to interpret the whole novel as a discourse on slavery; others to see it as a commentary on the Regency Crisis of 1788–9, with Tom Bertram as Regent, Sir Thomas as the *de facto* absent King George III), they fall in love with the idea of putting on a play in the billiard-room. This should in no way be taken to imply that Jane Austen was high-mindedly against amateur theatricals: she enjoyed reading aloud, and it's likely she enjoyed reading plays as much as any other writing. The problem is not play-acting, as such, it's *who*'s doing the acting and *what* they're performing.

The crowd has been swelled by the arrival of the sublimely fatuous, 'Idle and expensive', Mr Yates, and it is he who, frustrated by the collapse of his theatrical party in

Cornwall, 'Could talk of nothing else' but the play he has been deprived of. He galvanizes the others into staging *Lovers' Vows* (1798), an adaptation of German dramatist August von Kotzebue's marginally scandalous *Das Kind der Liebe* (1780), or *The Love-Child*. Illegitimacy, destitution and forced marriage are the key elements of this drama, first performed in England in 1798, but it's not just the content which makes it unsuitable: it's the apportioning of the parts. In particular, Maria Bertram playing the fallen woman, with Henry Crawford as her son; and Mary Crawford as Baron Wildenhaim's pert daughter, destined for the pastor, on this occasion aptly played by Edmund Bertram. There is a dangerous eroticism in all this, as well as a self-evident embracing of falsehoods and pretence.

And there is a greater misrule in Mansfield Park itself, as the young people take command of the property, ordering up curtains and manhandling the fabric of the building, as well as its permanent staff, to create a space for their drama. 'Could Sir Thomas look in upon us just now,' says Mary Crawford, 'he would bless himself, for we are rehearsing all over the house.' The anarchy is so overwhelming that even Fanny Price finds herself drawn into it. She reads in rehearsal, she prompts, she is about to fill in for the suddenly called-away Mrs Grant – which leaves her with 'The tremors of a most palpitating heart'. She, the fixed centre of the novel, is about to be corrupted by the play-within-a-play that is *Lovers' Vows*. The whole episode is often terribly funny; but when Fanny is imperilled, we finally see the full seriousness of the problem. It is only the suitably stagy arrival of Sir Thomas, unexpectedly back from Antigua – where his business has been 'Prosperously rapid' – that puts a stop to the fun. Even the Crawfords realize that the party's over, and elect to go home, trying in vain to persuade Mr Yates, who 'Could not perceive that anything of the kind was necessary', to go with them.

Sir Thomas's return raises questions at the same time as it provides a solution to imminent moral danger. He is the head of the family and its fount of authority. But what does the family make of him? After all, when he leaves, the Bertram sisters find his absence 'Most welcome', given that 'Their father was no object of love to them'; and proceed to grant themselves whatever licence they please. Tom Bertram has always been a wastrel, high-handed and dissipated, with his 'Races and Weymouth, and parties and friends', squandering the general inheritance, and only behaving himself when his father is actually standing over him. And Edmund is so unsteady in his vocation, so little prepared for life, that he can, at the drop of a hat, fall for a woman who holds that 'A clergyman is nothing'. Their shortcomings are the product of – let's be frank – poor parenting: there is a void between Sir Thomas and his own children, a relationship built on chilly formalities, that is now yielding predictable results.

Conversely, who is Sir Thomas most pleased to see when he gets back? 'Where is Fanny?' he demands. And then, on perceiving her, he comes forward 'With a kindness which astonished and penetrated her'. Very well – the reader understands that Austen is building on Fanny Price's virtues and positioning her for more important work. The surprising thing is how her advance has crept up on us – from neglected nonentity to the apple of Sir Thomas's eye and it is evidence of the deep structure of *Mansfield Park* at work, that, with sudden hindsight, we should find the advance plausible, and even necessary.

Fanny, though, is not part of Sir Thomas Bertram's immediate family. The proper order of things is in danger of being compromised, if not turned upside down. What is this semi-foundling doing, usurping Sir Thomas's affections? Maria, in particular, is now desperate to get away both from her failed dalliance with Henry Crawford, and from her own stultifying father ('She must escape from him and Mansfield as soon as possible'). The solution? To hitch herself at once to Rushworth and depart for the fleshpots of Brighton and London. Sister Julia, who has also unsuccessfully been making eyes at Henry Crawford, decamps with them. 'Fanny's consequence increased on the departure of her cousins', but with Tom vanishing from the frame and Edmund still floundering over his feelings for Mary Crawford, Fanny's 'consequence' starts to become a burden. Time and virtue have transfigured her into the pretty creature who makes Henry Crawford's pulse race at the thought of her 'Soft skin'; while Sir Thomas's starchy interest spills over into a proper appreciation of her new grace when he speaks 'Of her beauty with very decided praise' just before the ball of Chapter Twenty-Eight. And yet this evolution into what ought to be a state of absolute rightness for any Jane Austen heroine – potential love object of an attractive and wealthy young man – is, in an inversion of the expected, fraught with hazards.

By this stage, with the bright young people off the scene and that source of entertainment lost, most modern readers will have adopted one of three possible positions. The first is that they will have failed to engage with Fanny Price at any level, (especially now that there is no one to come between us and her pieties) and the novel as a whole will be pretty much an unwelcome chore. On the other hand, they *may* respect Miss Austen's craft, her perennially clever dialogue, her ambitious structure – and still find it impossible to do any more than tolerate Fanny, with the result that the book can only ever be a partial success. Or they can accept Fanny as Jane Austen intends us to and wait, with cautious optimism, to see how the story develops. Great novels demand investment. If *Mansfield Park* is a great novel, there is only one way to find out.

Because Austen is now adding complexity to complexity. Not only has she, daringly, got Fanny entangled with Henry Crawford (sister Cassandra wanted her to marry the two off, a suggestion Jane didn't *quite* take up), she has introduced brother William into the mix: emblematic of true, unconditional, family love, and a reproach to the failures of the Bertram household. William is also an involuntary member of a three-way love tangle, symbolized in the amber cross which he has brought from Sicily and presented to Fanny, but which has no chain. Both Edmund and Henry Crawford give her something by which to hang it round her neck, but only Edmund's 'Perfectly simple and neat' gold chain proves small enough to fit. *And* Miss Austen has unflinchingly pursued the internal logic of the situation, by turning Sir Thomas, Fanny's protector, into her persecutor.

Sir Thomas has, of course, fallen for Henry Crawford's sinister plausibility, and is urging Fanny to marry him: 'Gladly would I have bestowed either of my daughters on him.' The bind this puts her in is some considerable way short of the rape Samuel Richardson depicts in *Clarissa* (1748), but it is menacing enough. And this from the man who has put a fire in her chill sitting-room – 'A fire! it seemed too much'. Not the least of it is that it leads her into that worst of sins, ingratitude: 'I must be a brute indeed, if I can be really ungrateful!' But there is a natural consonance between Sir Thomas's emotional tone-deafness and Henry Crawford's capacity for dissimulation (given an airing yet again in his homily on 'The eloquence of the pulpit', delivered right in the face of the ingenuous and freshly ordained Edmund) just as there is a connection between Fanny's honesty and her own capacity to appreciate the moods of others.

And we are *still* in Mansfield Park. Austen has contrived to revolve several stories around Fanny Price, still the fixed point in the uncertain world, still metaphorically seated on her park bench – without apparently feeling the need to vary the location or the steady temporal course of the narrative. Which makes her next step all the more audacious. By moving Fanny back to the bosom of her real family in their slatternly quarters at Portsmouth, she not only startles us with the tonal shift, she very nearly answers the question, *what point is the novel trying to make?*

Of all the twists in Jane Austen's novels, this – more than the sudden revelation of an illegitimate child, or a secretly contracted marriage – is about the most surprising, not least because it takes us right away from what we think of as Jane Austen's world. It drops us in an altogether parallel world, a fully realized and radically different, situation. The twist takes us into another kind of dramatic episode, and locates us in the frowzy sub-existence of the Prices. In this world,

Fanny's father pains her 'By his language and his smell of spirits'; two younger brothers slam the parlour door 'Till her temples ached'; her mother is 'Always busy without getting on, always behindhand and lamenting it, without altering her ways'; and 'Nothing was done without a clatter, nobody sat still, and nobody could command attention when they spoke.' The logic of the dramatic move becomes clear. Fanny is unable to stop herself from thinking about Mansfield Park, with its 'Elegance, propriety, regularity, harmony', and brooding on the gap that has opened up between herself and her old ways. 'Portsmouth was Portsmouth', she reflects; 'Mansfield was home.'

Is this just Fanny Price the prig, the snob, simply wishing she could be somewhere a bit nicer? Not entirely, because her visit to Portsmouth coincides with the final, frantic, shifts in the narrative – including Tom Bertram's illness (a moral punishment, a variation on Marianne Dashwood's fever in *Sense and Sensibility*), the collapse of the Rushworth marriage and Maria Bertram's disgrace and Julia Bertram's elopement with Mr Yates. The daring of Fanny's embittered return to the bosom of the Price family is only exceeded by the daring with which Miss Austen overturns all the established relationships back at the Park – except in this case, more is at stake than the mere sorting-out of a love interest. By the closing stages of *Mansfield Park*, two generations of superior gentry – the entire Bertram family, plus the Crawfords – have been thoroughly impugned and Fanny, full of the insights granted by her brawling relations, has become the daughter that Sir Thomas never had. She has also introduced her sister, Susan, into Mansfield Park as 'The stationary niece', consolidating her hold. This is, on the one hand, a likeable enough conclusion to the fairytale of Fanny Price's rise from poor relation to keeper of the family conscience; on the other hand, it is also something much more unsettling – a critique of the gentry, an attack on the spiritual and temporal failings of the ruling order.

As Sir Thomas examines the mess in which the final chapter leaves him, he concludes that his children 'Had never been properly taught to govern their inclinations and tempers, by that sense of duty which can alone suffice', and acknowledges Fanny as 'The daughter that he had wanted'. As with Elizabeth Bennet, there is a feeling that Fanny Price is given a special dispensation as one of Nature's aristocrats to leapfrog her way up the social order. Her piety, her sense of duty and gratitude, even her dislike of wanton 'improvement' to an existing structure (as seen in Henry Crawford's enthusiasm for knocking about the Parsonage at Thornton Lacey – 'The house must be turned to front the east instead of the north') are every bit as proper as the behaviour of the Bertrams and the Crawfords is improper. This shows either a radical intention on Austen's part to challenge the procedures of the ruling order, or, more likely, a conservative desire for the ruling order to take its job more seriously and get back to the principles that sustain it. And as a manifesto – or at least, an agenda – this is at least as ambitious as everything else in *Mansfield Park*.

In the end, with *Mansfield Park*, Austen has taken us on a long and involved journey, far wider-reaching than anything in *Sense and Sensibility* or *Pride and Prejudice*. She has started out with a ten-year-old semi-orphan with no discernible talents or charms, tried her, elevated her, very nearly betrayed her and at last installed her as the spiritual head of a great country seat. Closer to Elinor Dashwood than Elizabeth Bennet, Fanny Price has experienced much, but changed very little, her undeviating virtue being her great – indeed, her only – strength. Issues of duty, family upbringing and the meaning of true affection have all been raised, along with the role of the landed classes. And there has been a real, worldly, sense of darkness at the heart of the story. Maria Bertram ends her days in banishment with Mrs Norris. Julia's elopement is unequivocally shameful – unlike Lydia Bennet's elopement in *Pride and Prejudice*, which she somehow brazens out – and cannot be repealed. And the Crawfords, although mildly tormented by regret and self-reproach, seem to get away more or less undamaged by the consequences of their idle viciousness.

It is a great achievement. But is that what this sometimes austere, sometimes bothersome, novel intends – to create a sense of achievement? Years go by and critics inspect Miss Austen's canon for something more than just romantic comedy: for signs of an ideology, for the rudiments of a larger argument. In *Mansfield Park*, they're most likely to find it – in a novel which is sometimes easier to fillet for abstractions than it is to enjoy as a novel; a novel which is never going to be loved.

Emma

Another quiz question: If *Pride and Prejudice* is Jane Austen's most popular novel, which is her greatest? Almost certainly *Emma*. How can we tell? After all, if there's one

salient fact about the book, it's that Emma Woodhouse
herself is a walking catalogue of prejudices, misjudgements
and wrong calls – the 'Heroine whom no one but myself
will much like', as Austen herself put it. The other great
thing about it is that, in the course of some four hundred
pages, nothing much happens. It is the last word in Austen's
'Little bit (two inches wide) of Ivory', which she worked
with 'So fine a brush'. It's either a masterpiece of
miniaturism, or a depiction of a world so narrow and
modest in its activities that one would have to be an
extreme Janeite, a real zealot, to get any pleasure out of
reading it. And then, even allowing for that, what happens
in *Emma* is what happens in all the other books –
romances come and go, mismatches are sorted out, the
central characters are tempered by events and they end the
book generally wiser than they were at the start. It is also
extremely densely written, a book in which it seems that
every word, every character, is equally weighted, equally
capable of interpretation in the larger scheme of the work,
a book which, even more than *Mansfield Park*, makes
demands on the reader.

All in all, it is not a promising recipe for a popular
masterpiece.

And yet this is the book (and writer) of which Sir Walter
Scott said, in 1816,

> We, therefore, bestow no mean compliment upon the
> author of *Emma*, when we say that, keeping close to
> common incidents, and to such characters as occupy the
> ordinary walks of life, she had produced sketches of such
> spirit and originality, that we never miss the excitation

which depends upon a narrative of uncommon events, arising from the consideration of minds, manners and sentiments, greatly above our own. In this class she stands almost alone.

Not many readers since then have disagreed with him. When English traveller and author Reginald Farrer wrote, 'While twelve readings of *Pride and Prejudice* give you twelve periods of pleasure repeated, as many readings of *Emma* give you that pleasure, not repeated only, but squared and squared again with each perusal, till at every fresh reading you feel anew that you never understood anything like the widening sum of its delights', his tone may be borderline hysterical, but his passion for the work is unmistakeable, and shared by many. And when Virginia Woolf famously observed that 'Of all great writers she is the most difficult to catch in the act of greatness', one's inclination is to add that her greatness is at its greatest in *Emma*, as is the sheer difficulty of pinning that greatness down, of saying exactly where it lives.

Austen didn't know for certain that it was Scott who had written such kind things about *Emma*, but she was nonetheless peeved that he'd neglected to mention *Mansfield Park*, only referring to *Sense and Sensibility* and *Pride and Prejudice* in his review; because it was *Mansfield Park* which represented her current thoughts on the way her art was developing, and it was *Mansfield Park* which allowed her to focus at length and in depth on a single, evolving story, much as she was to do in *Emma*. She was also galled that *Mansfield Park*'s original publisher had declined to produce a second edition; and that the edition which John

Murray *had* produced, was selling so slowly. She was peeved at having to dedicate the work to the Prince Regent, allowing herself to be described as 'His Royal Highness's Dutiful and Obedient Humble Servant'. And she was underwhelmed at being listed on the title page, yet again, as 'The Author of "Pride and Prejudice"'. All the same: the new work was so clever and so confidently written, that she could not help but hope for something good to come out of it.

The first thing in the book's favour, is that it reverts to a type of heroine that readers will, if not like, at least be entertained by. Emma Woodhouse is, in many ways, an evolution of Elizabeth Bennet – youthful, energetic, and beautiful. 'Can you imagine any thing nearer perfect beauty than Emma altogether – face and figure?' her former governess, Mrs Weston declares, adding that 'She is loveliness itself'. To this question the romantic interest, Mr Knightley, replies 'I love to look at her; and I will add this praise, that I do not think her personally vain.' Unlike Elizabeth Bennet, Emma is not only wealthy, but unencumbered by other siblings – her older sister having been married off to Mr Knightley's brother before the start of the book. 'Handsome, clever and rich, with a comfortable home and a happy disposition', is how Emma begins *Emma*: an erratically delightful companion, a mere twenty-one years old and, should we feel any uncertainty about this, eminently marriageable – despite her professed intention never to marry, and despite her 'Power of having rather too much her own way, and a disposition to think a little too well of herself'.

What's missing from the list are the higher virtues of

conscience and a sense of duty: qualities embodied in the stolid form of Mr Knightley – a composite of Mr Darcy and Colonel Brandon, well into his thirties, and, indeed, old enough to be Emma's father. Her real father has elements of Mr Bennet about him – a comparable self-interest, a similar gift for being marginal and annoying at the same time – but unnervingly refined by wealth and illness, 'A valetudinarian all his life', and with a terrible belief in the restorative powers of gruel. He is earmarked at the start as being 'Everywhere beloved for the friendliness of his heart and his amiable temper' – a view seemingly corroborated by other characters, with their references, among other things, to his 'Quaint, old-fashioned politeness'. It is hard, though – even impossible – for the modern reader to see Mr Woodhouse as anything other than a footling and inconsequential neurotic, an old woman, to whom Emma seems unaccountably attached. Luckily, Mr Woodhouse is not the only parental figure. In Mrs Weston, Emma has an alternative older sister who also manages the role of surrogate mother, 'Intelligent, well-informed, useful, gentle', and whose benignity warms the narrative at the same time as the lofty probity of quasi-father Mr Knightley cools it.

And those are the fixed elements of *Emma*'s universe. The rest of the players come and go, submitting themselves to clever Emma's scrutiny and ambitions. And so the business of the story starts.

The business being boredom. From the moment Miss Taylor becomes Mrs Weston, Emma is 'In great danger of suffering from intellectual solitude. She dearly loved her father, but he was no companion for her.' The other habitués of Hartfield, the Woodhouse home, are citizens like Mrs Goddard, a schoolmarm; and Mrs and Miss Bates, two pieces of impoverished gentility, who, when they turn up in order to pass the time, cause Emma to reflect that 'The quiet prosings of three such women made her feel that every evening so spent, was indeed one of the long evenings she had fearfully anticipated.' The future stretches ahead of her, full of 'Everyday remarks, dull repetitions, old news, and heavy jokes'. It is a sad employment of her talents, and what, really, could be more reasonable than that she tried to distract herself by match-making, by inventing narratives for others, by being 'An imaginist'?

Emma's circumstances are again apt to remind some readers of Jane Austen herself: clever, energetic, surrounded by the humdrum minds of provincial life, and evolving romantic fictions. Unlike Miss Austen, however, Miss Woodhouse does nothing but make mistakes, beginning with 'The natural daughter of somebody', the hapless Harriet Smith. Harriet is younger than Emma, a pretty ingénue (with just a hint of Fanny Price and her vague pieties) whose illegitimacy stands in bleak contrast to Emma's good breeding, her dim pliability an open invitation to Emma's need to meddle. Being both a snob and a fantasist, Emma at once dismisses the attentions that Robert Martin, the worthy farmer, directs at Harriet. Instead Emma steers her towards Mr Elton, the infinitely tastier vicar, 'A remarkably handsome man, with agreeable manners', and luckily not of such high birth that Harriet's lack of a father cannot be finessed. And so the romantic intrigues, involving Mr Elton, Mr Knightley, Harriet, Emma, the ineffable Frank Churchill and the mysterious Jane Fairfax, begin.

The tone and technique of Austen's narrative, likewise, become clear. One of her great gifts to prose fiction is her refinement of the free indirect style of narration – that sly, informal drift into the interior, sometimes exterior, voicings of a character, all of a piece with the authorial voice, but just distanced enough to be tonally distinct:

> Those soft blue eyes and all those natural graces should not be wasted on the inferior society of Highbury and its connections . . . Why had not Miss Woodhouse revived the former good old days of the room? – She who could do any thing in Highbury! . . . It was a wretched business indeed! . . . General benevolence, but not general friendship, made a man what he ought to be. – She could fancy such a man . . .

It is a technique both intimate and economical, moving you at once a little closer to the character without any unnecessary effort in the prose. In the case of *Emma*, the free indirect style takes you so close to the centre of Emma's thoughts and feelings, so often, that it very nearly takes over the story wholesale, transforming her into the unreliable narrator through whom all actions and personalities are mediated, leaving us, the readers, with the puzzle of deciding what's true and what's false, what's the product of her own partiality and what's an accurate interpretation of events.

At the same time (and by way of contrast) the world of Highbury, the little town around which the action revolves, is depicted with a new and remarkable degree of fastidiousness and fidelity. It's sometimes taken as the mark of a great

novel (Tolstoy's *War and Peace* being the daunting prime
example) that it should have no 'dead zones' and that
almost every character should be as fully realized and
illuminated as the next. Whether this is strictly true of
Emma or not, the fact is that Jane Fairfax, the horrid Mrs
Elton (with her undertones of Lucy Steele) and the
babbling Miss Bates ('A large basket of apples, the same
sort of apples, a bushel at least', and so on) are given so
much time and space that by the end we know them very
nearly as well as Emma, Knightley and Mr Frank Churchill. Just as we know the day-to-day realities of provincial
life, from Ford's haberdashery, to the Crown Inn, to
picture-framing, hair-curling, boiled eggs, the exigencies of
travel on badly made roads, stuffy dinner parties, tea, the
etiquette of paying a visit, the postal service, draughty
windows and teasing word-games. Scott's praise for
'Keeping close to common incidents, and to such characters
as occupy the ordinary walks of life' is justified in the way
Austen pays such attention to the commonplaces of her
world that the age of the Regency becomes familiar,
allowing us to make that strangest of imaginative leaps: into
another time.

The spaciousness Austen allowed herself in *Mansfield
Park* here becomes genuinely daring. She seems to be
drawing a life-class – as naturalistically as possible, and
with as few of the tropes of fiction as she can get away with.
Indeed, it would only take a moment of (extreme)
light-headedness to believe that the entire novel might pass
by in a diligent and acutely fashioned record of everyday
comings and going – with no ostensible plot at all. Even the
dialogue – of which there is an awful lot – seems faithful to

real speech, with its elisions, interrupted thoughts, half-finished sentences; as if Austen is so in love with the essence of things that she can't bring herself to hurry them along in order to make way for a mere plot.

But there is a plot, albeit one built on ironies and deceptions rather than high drama, overmastering emotions and formalized dialogue. And this plot revolves around Emma, and all the things she – naturally – gets wrong: starting with her wrong-headed sundering of Harriet's relationship with Robert Martin; going on to her doomed mismatch of Harriet with Mr Elton; her failure to spot Mr Elton's enthusiasm for her, Emma; her unfounded belief that Frank Churchill is in love with her (and her decision that she should be in love with him); her failure to see that Harriet has fallen for Mr Knightley; her failure to sense that Frank Churchill is actually attached to *someone else* (Jane Fairfax, as it turns out, previously bent on self-immolation as a governess); and her failure to anticipate Knightley's love for her.

It's the Frank Churchill story that draws the eye. Even though, near the halfway point, Emma's 'Resolution held of never marrying' Frank Churchill ('So long talked of, so high in interest', a creature of myth, very nearly), he is nonetheless in the centre of the frame, and there is 'Nothing to denote him unworthy of the distinguished honour which her imagination had given him; the honour, if not of being really in love with her, of being at least very near it, and saved only by her own indifference'. We know that, on this occasion, the money side of Emma's future has been taken care of by her past; but the question of marriage is still there, as intractable as ever.

Who or what, though, is Frank Churchill? The son of Mr Weston, brought up by a well-to-do uncle and aunt, again in the manner of Edward Austen Knight, Frank Churchill remains invisible for a surprisingly long time. His arrival in the book is delayed and delayed, until his persistent non-appearance becomes a piece of comedy in its own right; only brought to an end with his arrival, well into the second volume of the novel. He turns out to be 'A *very* good looking young man' – a mark of unreliability in Austen's scheme of things, compounded by his taste for fun ('They ought to have balls there' – the faded Crown Inn – 'at least every fortnight throughout the winter') and apparent personal frivolity ('Emma's very good opinion of Frank Churchill was a little shaken the following day, by hearing that he was gone off to London, merely to have his hair cut.'). Worse still, he plays up to Emma – 'Oh! Miss Woodhouse, why are you always so right?' – *and* he arouses Mr Knightley's suspicions. Mr Knightley has already scorned the idea of Frank Churchill – 'What! at three-and-twenty to be the king of his company' – even before Emma shows him one of Frank's letters, inviting him to admire the fineness of the handwriting, to which he at once replies, 'I do not admire it'. And why not? 'It is too small – wants strength. It is like a woman's handwriting.' The clincher, however, comes a few chapters later, with Mr Knightley's dismissive 'Hum! Just the trifling, silly fellow I took him for.'

The temptation, then, is to consign Frank Churchill to that now-familiar subset of plausible lotharios, containing Willoughby, Wickham and Henry Crawford, and await the catastrophe. But Austen is wily: we have already had one good-looking man go to the bad, in the form of Mr Elton.

Like his fictional predecessor Mr Collins, he has blurted out his longings to Emma; unlike Mr Collins, he has not only lit himself up with Dutch Courage, having 'Drunk wine enough to elevate his spirits', he has also made a pass at her in a carriage – 'Her hand seized – her attention demanded, and Mr Elton actually making violent love to her'. Furiously rebuffed, he has then, Collins-like, gone off in search of a more willing victim, which he has found in the form of Miss Augusta Hawkins, with her near enough £10,000 and her galling manner. But we can't have two such wanton operators in the space of one novel. Frank Churchill, therefore, must be more than he at first seems. At the same time, because this is *Emma*, Frank Churchill may turn out to be more than he seems, but he will not turn out to be what we might have expected. A younger Jane Austen would have been content to keep him entangled as some kind of love interest – which is clearly how Emma herself continues to see him, after several chapters of comings and goings: 'If he, who had undoubtedly been always so much the most in love of the two, were to be returning with the same warmth of sentiment which he had taken away, it would be very distressing.' But the older, shrewder, Austen has a different vision to convey; and she uses two of the lowlier, less-regarded characters to convey it.

Poor, dithering, Harriet Smith is one. The pathos of the scene in which she reveals to Emma the scrap of court plaster and the stub of pencil, relics of Mr Knightley that she has kept in an act of devotion to him, is heartbreaking. But it is also hedged about with uncertainty – Emma, needless to say, misconstrues who the object of Harriet's affections actually is – until a later scene in which Harriet makes it clear even to the purblind Emma, redoubling the pathos of her situation, and setting Emma's feelings in a spin as she does so. The revelation that it all stems from 'Mr Knightley's coming and asking me to dance, when Mr Elton would not stand up with me; and when there was no other partner in the room', has a sadness and a helplessness about it that touch us more than many of Fanny Price's sorrows in *Mansfield Park*, as well as locating the morality of the book in an unexpected quarter, at one remove from the more privileged, more vital, actors.

It's a trick that Austen pulls off twice. The cardinal scene on Box Hill, the excursion in the sunshine that turns sour, shows her at her most cunning. Quite apart from her game-playing with language – Emma and Frank Churchill's behaviour 'Must have had such an appearance as no English word but flirtation could very well describe. "Mr Frank Churchill and Miss Woodhouse flirted together excessively." They were laying themselves open to that very phrase' – she is at her steeliest, most candid and most acute in describing the jaded sensations of the day-trippers. 'There was a langour, a want of spirits, a want of union, which could not be got over', she says of the party as a whole; and of Emma in particular, it was 'Not that Emma was gay and thoughtless from any real felicity; it was rather because she felt less happy than she had expected. She laughed because she was disappointed'. The sense of dissatisfaction builds, made worse rather than better by flirtatious teasing and arch little word-puzzles. And it is in the middle of this brittle and frustrating atmosphere that Emma forgets herself and is heartlessly rude to innocent, garrulous, Miss Bates, who has made up the numbers of the party.

In the great scheme of things, this ought not be such a terribly big deal. Miss Bates is mortified; but an apology, one might imagine, should be enough to restore relations. Only Miss Bates means more than that. Mr Knightley, stung into action by Emma's callousness, rebukes her by specifically recalling the social distance between her and Miss Bates: 'She is poor; she has sunk from the comforts she was born to; and, if she live to old age, must probably sink more. Her situation should secure your compassion. It was badly done indeed!' It is a profound criticism, one that, through the instrument of Miss Bates, situates Emma's emotional fantasizing in real life, in society, linking personal, specific actions to social, moral behaviour. And it is from that point on, the Miss Bates moment, that Emma determines to mend her behaviour; while her world starts to fall apart around her. Life cannot be lived as a romantic fiction; and romantic fiction must have larger concerns than the whimsicalities of the young.

Of course, Emma's translation from spoilt meddler to sadder, more tolerant human being, only carries any weight if we can still find it in ourselves to care about her. Another small triumph for Miss Austen: she sustains our sympathies throughout the process. How can we gauge Emma's sincerity? In the alacrity with which she goes to make amends with Miss Bates, for a start. Having spent an evening of contrition, brooding on her 'Scornful, ungracious' self, and that morning on Box Hill, 'More completely misspent, more totally bare of rational satisfaction at the time, and more to be abhorred in recollection, than any she had ever passed', she heads off to Miss Bates's home, where she cheerfully puts up with a torrent of trivia from Miss Bates herself, every word adding to her sense of 'Dreadful gratitude'. From there on, she must suffer the discovery of Frank Churchill's covert relationship with Jane Fairfax – another of the unconsidered, demanding her place in the scheme of things – and the revelation of Harriet Smith's hopeless love for Mr Knightley. This is Emma's fever, her penitential suffering.

And she suffers, as it were, well. 'She saw it all with a clearness which had never blessed her before', is how Emma reacts to the Harriet Smith news; and the sense of humiliation that then overwhelms her is described in properly exacting detail. 'Till now that she was threatened with its loss, Emma had never known how much of her happiness depended on being *first* with Mr Knightley, first in interest and affection', is how Austen puts it, disappointing any progressive-minded readers who might have hoped that, unlike all Jane Austen's other heroines, Emma would have had enough money, position and aversion to marriage not to feel that her life could only be made complete by the addition of a man. She dwells on the wrongs Emma has done Jane Fairfax, too, culminating in a celebrated piece of phrase-making, in which all of Nature conspires to express Emma's wretchedness:

> The evening of this day was very long, and melancholy, at Hartfield. The weather added what it could of gloom. A cold stormy rain set in, and nothing of July appeared but in the trees and shrubs, which the wind was despoiling, and the length of the day, which only made such cruel sights the longer visible.

Indeed, 'The same loneliness, and the same melancholy' persist into the next day, as if she is doomed to live a twilight life as the consequence of her own wrong-headedness. Until, that is, the sun at last comes out, 'It was summer again', and Emma can think about rejoining the world. Which is as important, in its way, as the long process of self-discovery and self-reproach: her resilience, her capacity to return to life, are what make her worthy of our affection, just as much as her intelligence and playfulness. Austen knows that without this quiddity, we'd be left with not much more than a socially smarter Fanny Price, mournful and incomplete. It also means that when Mr Knightley so touchingly claims his prize – 'Most beloved Emma' – he is getting a proper reward, after all the feints and dissimulations; he is getting the real Emma. And in case we are in any doubt as to the rightness of this crucial scene – Mr Knightley's fateful avowals – Miss Austen closes it with one of her humorous throwaways, just to let us know that all is well: 'If he could have thought of Frank Churchill then, he might have deemed him a very good sort of fellow.'

So the end of the book resembles the end of any Jane Austen novel, with lessons painfully learned, the virtuous rewarded, the spectacle of a proud man bending over backwards to demonstrate his fealty to his new love (in this case, Mr Knightley moving in with the spavined Mr Woodhouse, just to keep him happy) and a clutch of marriages. But the final scenes of *Emma* are unlike those of its predecessors in at least one important respect. The moral landscape is ambiguous, full of relativisms and grey areas. Where are the villains, and where are their punishments?

Where is the virtuous heroine – Jane Fairfax? What actual wrongs have been committed? We have been taken on a very subtle kind of journey, one in which human nature, with all its shades of understanding, has been the prime object of interest – nothing larger or more dramatic, no good and evil, no outlandish pride and prejudice.

One of the things which annoys the kind of people who get annoyed by Jane Austen, is her apparent lack of interest in the history of the time – this age of revolution, war, social and economic change. Why does it always have to be so small-scale? Why can she not tackle something big, something more Dickensian in scope? But Miss Austen is never so vulgar as to be a mere big-picture historian: she is a chronicler of relationships. Which is why we still read her. And which is why, by the end of *Emma*, we are obliged to stand back and admire her artistry at its most searching and refined – 'Rich,' as David Lodge puts it, 'in that faultless observation of motive and behaviour and speech habits for which Jane Austen has always been justly admired'.

Persuasion

Persuasion is a novel that tends to attract one-word epithets, as if this final novel in Jane Austen's career is particularly susceptible to being summed up in one conclusive term. For many readers, it is 'autumnal'; for others, 'mellow'; 'bitter' and 'worldly' are terms that also crop up. Hedged about by the circumstances of its composition and publication, it is a novel that puzzles almost as much as *Mansfield Park* – but without any Emma waiting to make good the puzzlement, to redeem the doubt. 'Puzzling' might well be another handy adjective.

Jane Austen began *Persuasion* in 1815, straight after finishing *Emma*; but she was already ill, slowly declining towards death. Why is *Persuasion* her shortest book? Not least because she didn't have the time to write a longer one. Also, one suspects, because *Emma* had exhausted her, had been her defining work, and had left her with not much more to say on the subject of young people, feisty heroines, romantic misunderstandings and hard-won realizations. She also wanted to say something about a slightly older generation, something closer to herself – nearly forty years old – not an Emma, but a spinster in a quiet way of life. It is, in fact, a signal problem with *Persuasion* that it is so difficult to read without seeing Jane herself throughout the book. There is a sense of leave-taking about it that may have nothing much to do with the novel itself and everything to do with what we know of Miss Austen: in pain, weary, never finding the time for a final revision of the text, never definitively naming it – *Persuasion* being tacked on after her death by brother Henry.

The Elliot daughters, Elizabeth and Anne, could indeed both do duty as Austen surrogates – Elizabeth, the older, standing in for Cassandra, with Anne taking the place of Jane (both Jane and Anne, of course, capable pianists). The difference being that while Jane and Cassandra give the impression of being indivisible, two parts of the same entity, the Elliots are carefully rendered as distinct beings. Elizabeth, the older at twenty-nine, may be staring disappointment anxiously in the face ('She felt her approach to the years of danger, and would have rejoiced to be certain of being properly solicited by baronet blood within the next twelvemonth or two'), but she still has her looks and

her bearing, as we can tell from Austen's quietly conde-
scending 'It sometimes happens, that a woman is handsomer at twenty-nine than she was ten years before . . . It
was so with Elizabeth.'

Anne, conversely, is a lost cause. 'A few years before,
Anne Elliot had been a very pretty girl, but her bloom had
vanished early'; now, 'She was faded and thin', and, despite
possessing 'Elegance of mind and sweetness of character',
is 'Nobody with either father or sister: her word had no
weight; her convenience was always to give way – she was
only Anne.' Her destiny is always to submit to wayward
ambitions of Sir Walter Elliot, her father, and pay heed to
that old family friend, Lady Russell, who is also her
godmother.

Keen-eared readers will by now have sensed something
changed about Austen's prose: it sounds more direct, more
brusque, even in comparison with some of the more caustic
parts of *Sense and Sensibility* or *Pride and Prejudice*. Right
from the start, there is an unfamiliar feeling of irritability
in the long and satirical portrait of Sir Walter, for whom
'Vanity was the beginning and the end of Sir Walter Elliot's
character' and of whom 'Few women could think more of
their appearance than he did'. This abruptness continues
throughout the narrative – whether in the form of Mrs Clay
('Mrs Clay had freckles; and a projecting tooth, and a
clumsy wrist'), the memory of the Musgroves's son, lost at
sea ('Thick-headed, unfeeling, unprofitable Dick Musgrove') and even in Captain Wentworth's partiality for the
Laconia ship ('How fast I made money in her'). A younger
Jane Austen might have been just as brutal in her private
correspondence ('She appeared exactly as she did in

September, with the same broad face, diamond bandeau, white shoes, pink husband and fat neck', she wrote of Mrs Blount, in 1800) but in her fiction would have turned these ideas more elliptically, framing them in reported speech or sanitizing them with an authorial footnote of some kind. But not here.

Is *Persuasion* the product of haste? Or something else? For Virginia Woolf, a shrewd enough critic, this abruptness is a sign, not of an impending end, but of a change in the author's creative intentions. 'There is,' she says in her essay *Jane Austen at Sixty*,

> ... a peculiar beauty and a peculiar dullness in *Persuasion*. The dullness is that which so often marks the transition stage between two different periods. The writer is a little bored. She has grown too familiar with the ways of her world; she no longer notes them freshly. There is an asperity in her comedy which suggest that she has almost ceased to be amused by the vanities of a Sir Walter of the snobbery of a Miss Elliot.

Woolf then gets carried away by the idea of Austen surviving her illness, becoming properly acclaimed as a writer, spending more time in London being a celebrity and then writing about *that*: which tells us more about Mrs Woolf's own social ambitions than anything else. But still. Her take on *Persuasion* is plausible – Austen is clearly impatient with the old formula, and is trying out some changes.

For a start, her heroine, even though set in the mould of a patient, passive Elinor Dashwood or Fanny Price, is not

only relatively old, but has had her great romance before
the book even begins. Anne Elliot has actually met the
young Captain Wentworth nearly eight years earlier, at
which point 'They were gradually acquainted, and when
acquainted, rapidly and deeply in love.' He is young, just
at the start of his career, and penniless. By the time they
meet again, their circumstances, as well as their ages, have
become pretty nearly equivalent – in contrast to the
age/fortune discrepancies that exist between Marianne
Dashwood and Colonel Brandon, Elizabeth Bennet and Mr
Darcy, and Fanny Price and Edmund Bertram. Unlike
these predecessors, Anne and Wentworth could marry
without any undue loss of face on either part.

But they don't, because in its springtime, Sir Walter
Elliot has deemed their love affair 'A very degrading
alliance', while Lady Russell, who has been *in loco parentis*
since the death of Lady Elliot, advises Anne to drop the
liaison altogether, calling it 'Indiscreet, improper, hardly
capable of success, and not deserving it'. Anne – very
correctly – obeys, Captain Wentworth goes off to make his
fortune at sea, and time more or less stands still for Anne:
'No one had ever come within the Kellynch circle, who
could bear a comparison with Frederick Wentworth, as he
stood in her memory'. Like Fanny Price, she becomes
something of a character in a fairytale; unlike Fanny, she
declines instead of ripening, and her story is all about
recovering a lost arcadia, rather than discovering a new one.

So retrospection runs through *Persuasion* – not just in
memories of the failed relationship between Anne and
Wentworth, but in the melancholy of Captain Benwick's
inability to forget his lost love, Fanny Harville; in the even

sadder Mrs Smith's descent into penury at the hands of Mr Elliot ('We were a thoughtless, gay set, without any strict rules of conduct. We lived for enjoyment. I think differently now; time and sickness, and sorrow, have given me other notions'); in Wentworth's tales of naval adventure, and, quite separately, on the occasion when he catches Anne's eye as if to say, 'Even I, at this moment, see something like Anne Elliot again'; in Sir Walter Elliot's need to define himself by reference to his ancestors ('He could read his own history with an interest which never failed'); in Lady Russell's 'Pleased contempt, that a man who at twenty-three had seemed to understand somewhat of the value of an Anne Elliot, should, eight years afterwards, be charmed by a Louisa Musgrove'; and in the gloomy realization that, for both Anne and Captain Wentworth, 'Former times must undoubtedly be brought to the recollection of each; *they* could not but be reverted to'. The persistent, insistent, present of *Emma* is nowhere to be found in *Persuasion*, where so much is hedged about by history.

People are older in *Persuasion* than they are in *Emma*; they have done things with their lives. The various naval personnel who crop up in the course of the novel not only turn it into an open letter of appreciation to Austen's brothers, Frank and Charles, they introduce an unaccustomed note of worldliness to the story, quite unlike anything seen in her earlier stories. Wentworth's fortune – a really substantial one, at £25,000 – is prize money gained by the ferocious endeavour of capturing enemy ships during the Napoleonic Wars. The entertaining business of old built sloops and navy lists cannot quite disguise the underlying truth that life in the Navy was a terribly hard affair, not just because of the physical depredations it wrought on all classes of servicemen (as the foppish Sir Walter puts it, 'They are all knocked about, and exposed to every climate, and every weather, till they are not fit to be seen'); but because it was so dangerous. When *Persuasion* ends with the freshly married Anne's happiness only compromised by what might be expected of Wentworth in some later conflict – 'The dread of a future war all that could dim her sunshine' – we realize that we have strayed a long way from small-town society and the marriage game, and that Austen really is looking out to the greater world, glancing at politics and history, just as her critics wish she would.

And Anne is, at this point, *married*. Admittedly the great event slips past in the penultimate paragraph of the novel, but she nonetheless does what no other Austen heroine manages – she translates an engagement into an achievement. Because marriage *is* an achievement in *Persuasion*, or at least something that can be counted a success. Yes, there are the Musgroves, a typically unimpressive married couple (as are the Bennets, the Dashwoods, the Palmers, the Bertrams) with their beastly children; but there are also Admiral and Mrs Croft, not only estimable as individuals, but as paragons of the married condition. When the ebullient Louisa Musgrove cries out, 'If I loved a man, as she loves the Admiral, I would always be with him, nothing should ever separate us, and I would rather be overturned by him than driven safely by anybody else', it is an expression of confidence in the institution, not only for its social usefulness, but as an expression of continuing love. Which is then borne out by the Crofts' departure with

Anne in their little carriage, Mrs Croft 'Coolly giving the reins a better direction herself', in order to avoid a wooden post, 'and by once afterwards judiciously putting out her hand', to escape a couple of other dangers. Anne, far from complaining, is amused 'At their style of driving, which she imagined no bad representation of the general guidance of their affairs': and the author's approval is conferred by this proxy vote.

What effect do these shifts in emphasis, these new elements, actually have on the way we appreciate *Persuasion*? It *is* possible to read it as yet another variation on the basic Jane Austen love tangle, this time with Louisa Musgrove and Mr Elliot doing duty as the false leads, Mrs Musgrove, Sir Walter Elliot and Admiral Croft providing the elements of comedy, Mr Elliot (again) playing the plausible immoralist, the Harvilles striking a virtuous note, Sir Walter Elliot (again) as the delinquent father, and so on. But as we know, the authorial tone is different from the start; compounded by the fact that, for Miss Austen, there's not as much dialogue as usual, but instead an awful lot of expository prose. And although the levels of dialogue creep up as the story progresses, it is still – in comparison with *Emma* – a book full of narrative. And the narrative is mainly there to remind us of the different ways in which Anne Elliot can be made unhappy.

So the Elliots are forced, as a consequence of Sir Walter's financial incompetence, to move out of Kellynch Hall, the family seat, and rent it to Admiral and Mrs Croft. Anne finds herself billeted with the Musgroves, where her modesty and tractability make sure she gets taken for granted. Captain Wentworth, the Admiral's brother-in-law, fortuitously reappears in Anne's life, spending much of his time actively in search of a wife possessed of 'A strong mind, with sweetness of manner'. Faded Anne has to watch as the Musgrove girls fall over themselves to catch his eye, while she is reduced to the level of home entertainer, strumming the piano for an impromptu dance: 'And though her eyes would sometimes fill with tears as she sat at the instrument, she was extremely glad to be employed, and desired nothing in return but to be unobserved.'

Clergyman Charles Hayter arrives and makes a match with Henrietta Musgrove, but not before we learn that the other Charles – Musgrove – is believed to have wooed Anne. 'I wish she had accepted him,' declares Louisa, overheard apparently trysting with Wentworth, 'We should all have liked her a great deal better.' Austen then has her add that it was Lady Russell who 'Persuaded Anne to refuse him', parcelling up an entire sub-order of misconceptions in one short scene, before Anne is spirited away to Lyme Regis ('The young people were all wild to see Lyme') where the Harvilles and the unhappy Captain Benwick are introduced to the plot. Louisa Musgrove then nearly dashes out her brains by playfully leaping from the Cobb, and a note of melodrama rings out for the first time in several of Austen's novels, with Mary Musgrove's shrieks of 'She is dead! She is dead!' and Captain Wentworth staggering against a wall and yelling 'Oh God! Her father and mother!'

But no matter, because Louisa emerges from danger – about as expeditiously as Marianne Dashwood, in *her* medical emergency, although somewhat reduced in person-ality – and before we know it, we are in Bath (Anne, like

Miss Austen, 'Persisted in a very determined, though very silent, disinclination for Bath') and surrounded by a fresh arrangement of faces: Lady Russell, Sir Walter, the mysterious Mrs Clay, Colonel Wallis, Mrs Smith, Mr Elliot, Miss Carteret and Lady Dalrymple. Wentworth's apparent closeness to Louisa Musgrove is sequentially echoed by Anne Elliot's proximity to, and disillusionment with, Mr Elliot; while Lady Russell's ill-judged first persuasion of Anne not to marry Wentworth is echoed by her equally ill-judged certainty that she *should* marry Mr Elliot. There are some nicely vituperative glances at Bath life: in the preferences of the Elliots, 'Whose evening amusements were solely in the elegant stupidity of private parties'; and in the arrival of Lady Dalrymple at a concert, where '"Lady Dalrymple, Lady Dalrymple," was the rejoicing sound'. And there is a pleasing tension between the opaque Mr Elliot and the increasingly attractive Anne ('Very pretty, when one comes to look at her', as an anonymous onlooker remarks) to keep us beguiled.

But some readers will by now be pining for the shapely restraint of *Emma*, or even *Mansfield Park*. Why, one might ask, are there so many characters? For such a short novel, it teems with names. And why is Miss Austen rummaging around in her own literary back yard for such standbys as the life-threatening illness, and the handy revelation of a character's depraved past? Is it justifiable authorial hurry? Is it a loss of nerve? Is it symptomatic of Virginia Woolf's 'Transition stage'? There is an uneasy sense that she is not in command of her materials in the way we know she can be.

Or is it because, of all her novels, this is the one in which the ending is as important as the rest of the story, and she is impatient to get to it? As a rule, the concluding chapters of a Jane Austen novel are a way of rounding up any stray details and making sure that the virtuous get their rewards. They seem to grip her imagination less than anything else – and why should they? After all, the really interesting material has been dealt with. But *Persuasion* starts with a different premise: unlike Elizabeth and Darcy, or Fanny and Edmund – whose relationships are left to fulfil themselves, or not, in the abstraction of the future – Anne and Wentworth have to return to a state of prior happiness. They don't acquire much in the way of fresh understanding about themselves in the course of the book, except, possibly, to have more confidence in their own intuitions. They need to revert.

Which means that they have more ground to cover, rather than less. When Wentworth writes to Anne, 'I am half agony, half hope. Tell me that I am not too late, that such precious feelings are gone forever', the task he yearns to set himself involves rebuilding and reaffirming, rather than a relatively straightforward headlong plunge into whatever tomorrow might bring. It is complex. Also delicious, if it can be made to come right: and this is the treat which Jane Austen allows herself – to enjoy that situation in which, yes, 'It is something for a woman to be assured, in her eight-and-twentieth year, that she has not lost one charm of earlier youth.' Indeed, as she goes on to point out on behalf of her heroine, 'The value of such homage was inexpressibly increased to Anne by comparing it with former words, and feeling it to be the result, not the cause of a revival of his warm attachment'.

What do we make of the fact that, miraculously, both Wentworth and Anne have managed to overcome the malign effects of 'What persuasion had once done'? Do we yield to the impulse to see this as Austen's imaginative response to the dissuasion of Tom Lefroy, all those years ago? Do we see it as a note to herself as a writer – to remain steadfast, whatever compromises she might have endured, however much her books were outsold by Maria Edgeworth or Sir Walter Scott, however tricky it was to secure any attention for *Mansfield Park*? Is it no more than a sentimental fantasy? Is this not the most self-indulgent conclusion Miss Austen could invent: 'How should a Captain Wentworth and an Anne Elliot, with the advantage of maturity of mind, consciousness of right, and one independent fortune between them, fail of bearing down every opposition'? Whatever one makes of it, it is an ending unlike her other endings; and it is framed by the knowledge that, even though she had made a start on the fragment known as *Sanditon*, the last words of *Persuasion* are effectively her epitaph. And for Mrs Woolf, an invitation to speculate.

Northanger Abbey

If there is something conveniently literary about Jane Austen's last completed work, *Persuasion*, being parcelled up with her first, *Northanger Abbey*, in one edition and sold by John Murray as being 'By the Author of "Pride and Prejudice", "Mansfield-Park", &c.' – thus compacting her entire career as an author into two shortish bookend novels – then it is not a convenience that Miss Austen would have appreciated. After all, *Northanger Abbey*, as she herself

notes in her *Advertisement* at the start of the book, was
originally completed in 1803, having begun life as *Susan* in
the 1790s – before being obscurely stifled by Crosby &
Cox for more than a decade. 'That any bookseller,' she
observes, 'should think it worth while to purchase what
he did not think it worth while to publish, seems extraordinary.' Such dilatoriness meant that when *Susan* (or *Miss
Catherine*, as it was briefly known) was at last earmarked
for publication in 1817, 'Some observation is necessary
upon those parts of the work which thirteen years have
made comparatively obsolete.'

The parts Austen was particularly concerned with were
'Places, manners, books and opinions', but the contemporary reader, regarding everything as a matter of period, is
hardly going to worry about what may or may not have
seemed stale in 1816. More likely, they will wonder where
to locate their interest in the book itself – given that while
it looks an awful lot like a Jane Austen novel, it is clearly
being driven forward by an agenda, or at least a governing
set of interests, which can't help but remind us that
Northanger Abbey comes not that long after Austen's
Juvenilia, with all their love of parody and literary wise-
cracking, and their teenage lack of engagement with the real
world.

Readers may also be scratching their heads in perplexity
over its reputation as a gothic novel, or, at least a parody of
one. The gothic novel was a product of the late eighteenth
century, an extension of the sentimental novel, a distant
relation of the Romantic Movement, and something of a
freak in the general development of the novel as a literary
form. Horace Walpole's *The Castle of Otranto* (translated

'From the Original Italian of Onuphrio Muralto') was probably the first gothic novel, appearing in 1764; Ann Radcliffe's *The Mysteries of Udolpho*, of 1794, was probably the most successful; and Matthew Lewis's *The Monk*, of 1796, probably the most notorious. This last begins in a state of frenzied over-excitement and works its way up from there. By the end of the book, one character has been raped in a crypt by the Monk, Ambrosio, (surrounded by 'Rotting bones and disgusting figures', the Monk feasts upon Antonia's 'Swelling breasts, round, full, and elastic!'); while another character, Agnes, has been entombed with the corpse of her child ('It soon became a mass of putridity, and to every eye was a loathsome and disgusting Object; To every eye, but a Mother's'). To round things off, Lucifer himself makes an appearance in the final chapter. Lewis wrote the book in the space of a couple of months; and was nineteen years old when he did so, which may account for much.

The Monk is evidently a long way removed from *Northanger Abbey*. The nearest Austen gets to actual gothic is in Catherine Morland's fit of the vapours at Northanger, where 'A high, old-fashioned black cabinet' in her bedroom looks promising, but turns out to contain a laundry list and a farrier's bill; and where a spooky doorway, behind which General Tilney's deceased wife may or may not lie, conceals nothing more than a pleasant apartment, into which 'The warm beams of a western sun gaily poured through two sash windows!' When Henry Tilney catches her in the act of breaking into the apartment he tellingly enquires, 'Dearest Miss Morland, what ideas have you been admitting?'

Ideas being the key. In fact, the gothic component of

Northanger Abbey is just one part of a larger design, which considers literature of all sorts, and the correct response to it. This is a bookish novel, written by a bookish young woman, and the gothic strain is a nod to what was fashionable at the time of composition, back at the turn of the century, rather than a sign of any great attachment to the gothic genre. It is a book about books. Accordingly, the story begins with what sounds like a typically Jane Austen declarative, given a curiously self-referential twist: 'No one who had ever seen Catherine Morland in her infancy, would have supposed her born to be an heroine'. And the idea of the 'heroine' – this consciously literary creature – sets the tone for the next few pages, in which Miss Morland 'Read all such works as heroines must read', including Pope, Gray, Thompson and Shakespeare. And, 'Though she could not write sonnets, she brought herself to read them'. At the end of which investment of time – 'Something must and will happen to throw a hero in her way'. The hero, as it transpires, being Henry Tilney.

How do we feel, though, about the prospect? This is a rather different Jane Austen from the one we have become familiar with. This is Austen the tyro, so keen to impress with her cleverness that she is in danger of sounding arch, rather than simply mischievous. This is Austen writing to make a point about someone's relationship with reading, rather than someone's relationships with other people. This is also Austen writing with youthful cynicism, under the impression that it sounds worldly. And if we have any doubts as to how worldly she wants to sound, these are dispelled once she has located the action of the novel among the jaded exhibitionists of Bath, in Chapter Two.

Which is an oddity in its own right. Austen's settings are frequently like the physical descriptions she provides for her characters: suggestive, nominal. She prefers to hint, then let the dialogue and action do their work. But the Bath of *Northanger Abbey* is, by her standards, alarmingly specific. Before we know it, we are in the Upper Rooms, catching glimpses of the 'High feathers of some of the ladies'; then we are down in the Lower Rooms, and making the acquaintance of the Master of Ceremonies; then at the theatre, hoping to find the mysteriously attractive Henry Tilney; then at the Pump-room; then in the archway opposite Union-passage. She also declares that 'Every body acquainted with Bath may remember the difficulties of crossing Cheap-street at this point', a bold advertisement of the fact that she had first visited the city in 1797, before going on to comment on the rain, the umbrellas, the preferability of taking a chair rather than walking, the proximity of Bristol.

At the same time (and how could it be otherwise?), her prose has an eighteenth-century busyness about it that, from time to time, very nearly topples over into indecorousness. When the idiotic John Thorpe first makes his appearance, he sounds like something out of a Henry Fielding novel, with his horses and his carriages and his profanities – '"Oh! d—," said I, "I am your man"'; and '"Oh! d – it, when one has the means of doing a kind thing by a friend, I hate to be pitiful"'. The equally tiresome Isabella Thorpe could be one of Sheridan's noisier creations, exclaiming in the theatre, 'Oh! what would not I give to see him! I really am quite wild with impatience', which is followed by, 'Oh! horrid! am I never to be acquainted with him? How do you like my gown? I think it does not look amiss; the sleeves are entirely my own thought.' Henry Tilney, by way of contrast, though clearly tipped as the love interest, gets dangerously close to a kind of Georgian camp, especially in his early manifestations, 'Affectedly softening his voice', speaking 'With a simpering air' and taking a worrying interest in women's fashion: 'My sister has often trusted me in the choice of a gown. I bought one for her the other day, and it was pronounced to be a prodigious bargain by every lady who saw it. I gave but five shillings a yard for it, and a true Indian muslin.' Miss Austen herself gives in to the mood, describing how 'With smiles of most exquisite misery, and the laughing eye of utter despondency,' Isabella Thorpe 'bade her friend adieu and went on'; and that 'A fine Sunday in Bath empties every house of its inhabitants, and all the world appears on such an occasion to walk about and tell their acquaintance what a charming day it is.' It all sounds a bit odd: all of it obviously hers, but without the quiet irony or the moral seriousness we expect. It reminds us that this really is an early work.

But if the texture and tone of the writing are unfamiliar, at least the basic materials of the plot are of a piece with Austen's later novels. We have the heroine Catherine Morland, poised somewhere between Fanny Price and the warmer-blooded – and similarly self-taught – Marianne Dashwood. We have Henry Tilney, clergyman and romantic male lead, in the manner of Edmund Bertram or Edward Ferrars; and we have John Thorpe, a contrasting dunderhead pitched somewhere between John Yates and Robert Ferrars. We have Isabella Thorpe, an exploitative she-monster in the manner of Lucy Steele, Mary Crawford or Lydia Bennet. We have Mrs Allen, a middle-aged social fusspot not a million miles from Mrs Bennet; and we have General Tilney, a ruined tartar in the manner of Sir Thomas Bertram. We have the cast of a Jane Austen novel, in fact. What we don't have are the same organizing principles.

Which means that the first half of the book is marked principally by a sense of inertia. Catherine Morland is not shabby, like Fanny Price; nor reduced to genteel poverty, like Marianne Dashwood; nor affluent gentry, like Emma Woodhouse – but is unthreateningly well to do in a way which removes a possible source of drama before the book has even started. So she goes to Bath with the Allens, makes the acquaintance of Henry Tilney, the Thorpe family (including the pretty and coquettish Isabella and the bovine John), Henry's sister Eleanor Tilney, and, at last, General Tilney. All of which takes some thirteen chapters, without anything much happening, save a good deal of chit-chat and some foundation-laying for future romantic entanglements. Austen herself states, at the start of the thirteenth chapter, 'Monday, Tuesday, Wednesday, Thursday, Friday and Saturday have now passed in review before the reader; the events of each day, its hopes and fears, mortifications and pleasures have been separately stated, and the pangs of Sunday only now remain to be described, and close the week.' Clearly she is still full of enthusiasm. But we are starting to wonder when the happily discursive nature of the book will tighten up into something more determined – even as we nostalgically recall how much action Austen crammed into the opening stages of *Sense and Sensibility* and *Pride and Prejudice*; and as we conclude that she has made the beginner's mistake of too much writing, and not enough story-telling.

It keeps coming back to the literary imperative. This is what gives *Northanger Abbey* its distinctiveness, at the same time as it threatens to slow the narrative to a crawl. It just will not stop turning up – in Henry Tilney's positively eighteenth-century diction: 'I should no more lay it down as a general rule that women write better letters than men, than that they sing better duets, or draw better landscapes'; in Austen's over-attentiveness to setting the scene: 'They all three set off in good time for the Pump-room, where the ordinary course of events and conversation took place'; and, inevitably, in the discussion of other works of literature.

This varies: From Isabella Thorpe's tripping itemizations of what's fashionable – 'Midnight Bell, Orphan of the Rhine, and Horrid Mysteries. These will last us some time' – to John Thorpe's gormless revelation that 'I never read novels; I have something else to do' – to Eleanor Tilney's assertion that historians 'Display imagination without raising interest,' (with several pages of argument to follow) – to Austen's own aside, 'The advantages of natural folly in a beautiful girl have been already set forth by the capital pen of a sister author' (a reference to Fanny Burney's *Camilla*) – to Henry Tilney's naughty parody of gothic cliché, re-minding Catherine that while the rest of the family 'Snugly repair to their own end of the house,' innocent female gothic houseguests are invariably 'Conducted by Dorothy the ancient housekeeper up a different staircase, and along many gloomy passages, into an apartment never used since some cousin or kin died in it about twenty years before.'

The only thing that will create any real forward movement amid all these cultural nods and winks is Northanger Abbey itself: the embodiment, in Catherine's mind, of a literary reality; and as desirable as any human love interest. When she finally receives an invitation to stay, she can't believe her good fortune: 'Northanger Abbey! – These were thrilling words, and wound up Catherine's feelings to the highest point of exstasy.' Both she and her creator are in thrall to an idea. Unsympathetic critics might point out that there are two main structural problems with *Northanger Abbey*: it takes too long to get to the Abbey itself – a typical novice error, holding back an encounter for reasons of excessive partiality, not because the plot demands it; and when the move finally does come, it's ineptly articulated, and leaves the novel more or less broken in two.

Still, the consummation approaches, and Catherine must quit Bath, leaving very little decided – other than Isabella's implausible engagement to her brother James (along with a blithe insistence that 'The smallest income in nature would be enough for me. Where people are really attached, poverty itself is wealth', followed by a vulgar flirtation with Frederick Tilney and his 'Inferior' manners), and John Thorpe's horribly knowing invitation, 'Let me only have the girl I like, say I, with a comfortable house over my head, and what care I for all the rest? Fortune is nothing.' To which Catherine replies with an appalled 'We shall be very glad to see you at Fullerton, whenever it is convenient.'

Then she is off to have her preconceptions dismantled at Northanger Abbey, thirty miles away. It all starts as well as it possibly can, with a delightful ride in a curricle (carriage) with Henry Tilney – 'To be driven by him, next to being dancing with him, was certainly the greatest happiness in the world' – but this is naturally a prelude to unhappiness, as she insists on entangling herself in fictions. This is Austen's chance, at last, to have fun with the gothic genre, much as she used to have parodic fun in *Lesley Castle* and *Love and Freindship*, back at the start of the 1790's. Accordingly, Catherine's first night at the Abbey becomes a compendium of hand-me-downs, including, 'The night was stormy'; 'Catherine's heart beat quick'; 'Her knees trembled, and her cheeks grew pale'; 'Every blast seemed fraught with awful intelligence'; 'Hollow murmurs seemed to creep along the gallery'; and so on. This goes on for a few pages before Catherine falls asleep, wakes up the following morning to her bright, cheerful room, and discovers that the mysterious piece of paper from the sinister black cabinet is a laundry list.

After which, Austen begins to make her point: that human relationships contain more drama than any jaded fictional form, and that it is the job of the rest of the book to see Catherine Morland through the process of recognition that is at the heart of any Jane Austen novel; 'The visions of romance were over. Catherine was completely awakened'. And if Catherine *must* uncover an ogre in human form, a gothic entity, then General Tilney is that ogre.

Unlike Montoni in *The Mysteries of Udolpho*, or Ambrosio in *The Monk*, the General may begin appealingly enough, being 'Agreeable, and good-natured, and altogether a very charming man', to say nothing of 'Tall and handsome'. And he may be astonishingly solicitous when Catherine eats her breakfast in the Tilney house in

Milsom-street. But the clouds start to gather almost at once, as the General upbraids his older son for 'Laziness' in a manner 'Which seemed disproportionate to the offence'. Then, at Northanger Abbey itself, he starts to resemble the kind of person whose equilibrium can only be guaranteed by the extent to which he can unsettle everyone else. His invitation to show Catherine around the house and grounds turns into an ordeal of second-guessing, which leaves Catherine 'Anxious', and Eleanor Tilney 'Embarassed'. He continues a regime of oppressive solicitude towards Catherine, offset by a persistent tetchiness towards his own children, which only lightens when he actually leaves Northanger and goes to London. 'The happiness with which their time now passed,' Catherine notes to herself, 'made her thoroughly sensible of the restraint which the General's presence had imposed, and most thankfully feel their present release from it.' All of which comes to an abrupt end with the General's sudden decision to remove his family to Hereford and turf Catherine out at seven in the morning and send her home, unaccompanied, fending for herself for eleven hours, changing from one ruffianly public conveyance to another. 'He certainly is greatly, very greatly discomposed,' says Eleanor Tilney, 'I have seldom seen him more so.' Why? We don't know. We only know that the forlorn Catherine is obliged to tough it out, a 'heroine' in 'solitude and disgrace', and reflect that her present unhappiness is 'Mournfully superior in reality and substance' to the frights she pictured for herself when first coming to Northanger Abbey. The General 'Must be a very strange man', her parents speculate on her return home.

The crisis at last overcome, Austen wraps up the

narrative in the only way she knows how – by uniting the lovers in marriage (after Henry has been 'Open and bold' in his defiance of the General) with a flourish of, even by her standards, implausible plot resolution. In turn, the reader is provoked into an irresistible desire to interpret *Northanger Abbey* as an autobiographical coming-of-age, in which Jane Austen leaves behind her love of writing for its own sake and accepts that character must be the well-spring of plot; that a close observation of human nature will serve her better than a gothic lancet, or a creaking door. As Henry Tilney observes – trying to calm down an overwrought Catherine, paralysed at the head of a staircase – 'Consult your own understanding, your own sense of the probable, your own sense of what it passing around you'. It could almost be Jane Austen's critical conscience, telling her what to do next.

3

JANE AUSTEN'S REGENCY

The Regency

Strictly speaking, The Regency lasted from 1811 to 1820 – that is, from when The Regency Act came into effect, to the time when the Prince Regent finally ascended the throne as George IV. But the Prince managed to cast a much larger shadow than those nine years imply. This was in part thanks to the Prince's extravagant and excessive personality; in part due to all the anxieties that attended his father, George III, whose mental health had started to collapse at the end of the eighteenth century. The Regency Crisis of 1788, during which the King was temporarily incapable of being a monarch, very nearly saw the Prince of Wales formally installed as Regent. It was only because of the patchy recovery of the King's wits from 1789 onwards, that the transition from Prince to Prince Regent was delayed.

He had to wait until the Care of King During his Illness Act of 1811, before formally assuming the title of Regent.

George Augustus Frederick, the Prince, had therefore established his political centrality some twenty years before he actually became Regent. More than that – he had established a social tone, an atmosphere that coloured the whole period of his adulthood, leading most people to talk in a helplessly inclusive sort of way, of *The Regency Era*, stretching from the end of the eighteenth, to well into the nineteenth, century. How did he manage it? Well, there was a good deal of top-down influence, which started at Carlton House, the Prince's London base, and spread through politicians and the nobility, embracing architecture (about which he was especially passionate), theatre, fashion and the arts, and ending up, frankly, in the bedroom, where the Prince's complete lack of moral discipline delighted some, while scandalizing everyone else.

The Prince was a mess of vices and virtues. Known (not invariably) as The First Gentleman of Europe, otherwise 'Prinny', he was famously charming, clever, exquisitely well-mannered if the occasion suited him and highly cultured. George Canning praised 'The elegance of his address and the gentlemanliness of his manner'; his absolute support for the architect John Nash led to the creation of some of the finest urban spaces in England; the Duke of Wellington called him (with some equivocation, it has to be said) 'The most accomplished man of his age'; his tastes were extravagant, even preposterous, but he was nonetheless sincere about what he loved. He once wrote to Humphrey Repton, who had penned a fabulous new design for the Pavilion at Brighton, 'I consider the whole of this work as perfect and will have my part carried into immediate execution; not a tittle shall be altered – even you yourself shall not admit any improvement'. He even liked Jane Austen's novels.

The vices, though, are a lot easier to itemize, provided you have sufficient time and space. His financial incontinence alone is enough to boggle the imagination. Despite receiving a grant of £60,000, plus an annual income of £50,000, at the age of twenty-one, by the time he was twenty-four, he was already £270,000 in debt. Parliament bailed him out, the gift including a subvention to pay for the exquisite neoclassical remodelling he had made to Carlton House – 'The most perfect in Europe', according to Horace Walpole. This did nothing to moderate his tastes or his profligacy, and at the turn of the century, Parliament granted him another £65,000 followed by a further £60,000 just to tide him over. Nevertheless, by 1812, he was back in debt to the tune of £550,000, and clearly intending – now he was officially Prince Regent – to spend even harder than before.

What was he spending on, though? Everything, seems to be the answer: fabulous architectural schemes, wardrobes of clothes, stables full of race horses, food and drink on a staggering scale, plus women, gambling, oil paintings, partying, cronies and hangers-on. English caricaturists of the day – George Cruikshank and James Gillray probably the best-known – habitually drew him as a flushed, fat-thighed fop, either stuffing his face at the dinner-table, or panting over one of his costly mistresses. The mistresses were an even worse affront to public sensibilities than the squandering of money. Not only did he contract a clandestine morganatic marriage with Mrs Fitzherbert (by whom he may have had a number of children), he openly conducted affairs with (among others) an actress named Mary Robinson, the Countess of Jersey, and the Marchioness of Hertford. Forced into an official marriage with Princess Caroline of Brunswick in order to get his debts paid off in 1795, he went on to treat the Princess with scandalizing disrespect, siring a daughter by her – Princess Charlotte – before abandoning her to exile in Italy. Princess Caroline was, it must be said, not only plain, but dirty, vulgar, idiotic and bad-tempered. She spent a good deal of her time sticking pins into wax effigies of the Prince, intoning curses as she did so. She was, nevertheless, more popular with the British public than her husband, who, when he wasn't offending high-born foreign visitors such as the Grand Duchess of Oldenburg ('His much boasted affability is the most licentious, I may even say obscene, strain I have ever listened to'), was actually hissed at in the streets by a people which detested him.

Nor did he give much effort to politics. There was nothing much there to interest him, no sex, not much drinking and no opportunities to extend the limits of his connoisseurship. His interventions, as Prince Regent and subsequently as George IV, tended to be intemperate and principally motivated by a need for cash or by a dislike of the principle of Catholic Emancipation. As time went by, he got fatter, more reclusive and more eccentric, until he finally died in 1830, making way for his marginally more impressive brother, William IV. During the Prince Regent's life, the prestige of the British Monarchy collapsed, the public coffers were denuded and a tone of moral laxity was set by the ruling classes, which managed to shock and appal.

Yet the sweep of the decades from 1780 to 1830 can still be termed the Regency Era. Prince George may have been appalling as the effective head of the Royal Family, but he did establish the perfectly sound notion that art and culture could, and should, be present in every aspect of life; that it was right to be discriminating and to have a sense of the fine and the beautiful. Whatever else he did, the Prince Regent pursued the culture of the aesthetic with energy, taste, sincerity and someone else's money. It *was* an achievement.

The Regency Era co-existed with another great defining historical entity: the French Revolution, and everything that flowed from it. If 1789 saw the opening convulsions of the Revolution, it wasn't until 1799 – and Napoleon's seizure of power in the Coup of 18 Brumaire (9 November) – that the lineaments of the next fifteen years started to become clear. Bonaparte, having declared himself First Consul, then moved on to become Emperor Napoleon I in 1804. After this, much of Europe – and part of Russia – fell into a decade of war. This came not long after the initial decade of war mongering with Revolutionary France, in the course of which France seized Belgium and parts of Northern Italy, before having its fleet destroyed by Admiral Nelson at the Battle of the Nile (1–3 August 1798). In 1802, Britain and France signed the Treaty of Amiens, and the two nations enjoyed a year of peaceful relations before the Napoleonic Wars broke out in earnest, in 1803. At the time there would have been one or two Britons who remembered the last time the nation set out against a tyrannical French aggressor, who recalled Marlborough's campaigns against Louis XIV at Blenheim, Ramillies and Malplaquet and who must have been wondering why it all seemed to have started again.

But it did start, and the conflict dragged on from 1803 to 1815. The brief period of amity in 1802, in which the English reaffirmed their love of all things French ('Thousands of oddly dressed English flocked to Paris immediately after the war', noted one commentator) turned out to be a chimera, and the litany of historical moments began to compose itself – Trafalgar, The Peninsular War, Corunna, Austerlitz, Wagram, Borodino, the Retreat from Moscow, exile on Elba, Waterloo. And during the course of all this, Britain found itself accidentally at war with America. Orders in Council had subjected the whole of Napoleonic Europe to a trade blockade: this included trade with the United States – who, with the Chesapeake affair of 1807 still fresh in their minds, objected. So in 1812 they declared war on the British. This led to fighting on the American mainland (in Washington and New Orleans, most notably) and a number of naval skirmishes, before both parties wearied of the struggle and signed the Treaty of Ghent in 1814. When Napoleon at last fell, a year later, riotous celebrations broke out all over England, the Poet Laureate, Robert Southey, dashed off a poem to commemorate the victory at Waterloo and the Duke of Wellington found himself deified.

While all *this* was going on, domestic politics was throwing up such dynamic figures as Pitt the Younger (who became the youngest Prime Minister of Britain in 1783) and Quaker scientist Charles Fox; English literature was on fire with the Romantics – Samuel Taylor Coleridge, William Wordsworth, Percy Bysshe Shelley and John Keats; J. M. W. Turner was becoming the greatest painter England ever produced; Charles Babbage was dreaming of his first Difference Engine; Humphry Davy, Michael Farady and Edward Jenner were revolutionizing science; George Stephenson was revolutionizing transport. The war had caused food shortages, the Industrial Revolution was creating new worlds of startling wealth and terrible urban poverty, riots were commonplace, the abolition of the slave trade was becoming a reality, soldiers were stationed in camps along the south coast, the Empire was expanding and Britain was on the brink of becoming the world's superpower. Seen in précis, the age of the Regency was an almost impossibly exciting time.

But for Jane Austen? She had no time for the Prince Regent, despite being cajoled into writing a dedication to him – indeed, she preferred (if she had any preference at all) his dismal wife, Princess Caroline. 'I shall support her as long as I can, because she *is* a Woman, & because I hate her Husband', she declared in a letter to her friend Martha Lloyd. She had no particular feeling for scientific progress or the Industrial Revolution. She was not a political creature. Only the war with France makes any serious inroads into her narratives, and then her take on it is strictly personal, using it only as a background on which to paint the human details which interest her. Which is one reason why her novels have survived: the human experience, as opposed to the history lesson, never gets stale.

So. There was the Regency Era, and there was Jane Austen's Regency. Which consisted of what? What were the practicalities of ordinary life, as opposed to High Life, at that time? What kind of world did Mr Darcy, Miss Woodhouse, Fanny Price, Mr Bennet, actually inhabit?

I. The Home

Most of Jane Austen's modern readership lives in a town or city: that's how society has developed in the two hundred years since she began writing. There's a temptation to assume that the small, essentially rural communities that she described – with their squires, churches, inns, small-scale market towns – were already something of an anachronism; and that she chose those settings largely for artistic convenience.

But England at the start of the nineteenth century was still constituted very much like the England of the eighteenth century, even allowing for the arrival of the Industrial Revolution and the consequent explosive growth of the cities. Once you were outside London, Birmingham or Manchester, it was a farming landscape pretty much wherever you turned, and around eighty per cent of Britain's population of nine million would have had some sort of connection with agriculture. This might have entailed working as a farm worker or as a domestic servant, employed anywhere from a Big House to a moderate cottage; or as one of the higher economic entities – a farrier, a corn merchant, a factor, a publican. After that, one went from smallholder all the way up to the higher degrees of farmer, with, some way beyond, the squirearchy and the gentry. Jane Austen may have turned her back on the new urban realities, but it doesn't mean that the picture she painted was false or nostalgic. And the countryside was – especially in comparison with today's rural scene – densely populated.

Miss Austen, of course, comes from and concerns herself with, the lesser gentry: the 'middling classes', those ancestors of the middle class. The Dashwoods, the Bennets, the Morlands, even the Prices, are located somewhere in the same social class as the Austens, and, naturally enough, enjoy a more refined way of living than that suffered by the humble labourer, with his smoky cottage, his stone floor and his rude furnishings. Indeed, visitors to Austen's last home, in Chawton, can still get a reasonable sense of what a genteel, Bennet-style establishment must have looked like. And very pleasant it is.

Quite apart from the happy proportions of many of the rooms, with bits of furniture in the style of English furniture maker George Hepplewhite, the square piano, the touches of Scottish architect Robert Adam's classicism around the fireplaces, the usefully large sash windows and the comfortable beds, there are decorative elements which make the contemporary visitor feel pretty much at home. When the Austens made their great move to Bath there was much debate about whether or not to take the larger pieces of furniture with them: the beds were sent down, but Jane did not think 'It will be worth while to remove any of our chests of drawers; we will be able to get some of a much more commodious sort, made of deal, and painted to look very neat'. Clearly, furniture came and went, but the mood at Chawton is thoughtfully maintained, not just by the bigger stuff, but by framed pictures and prints; light, sprigged wallpaper; pieces of china. 'I had the pleasure,' she wrote, in 1811, 'of receiving, unpacking, and approving our Wedgwood ware. It all came very safely, and upon the whole is a good match, though I think they might have allowed us rather larger leaves, especially in such a year of fine foliage as this. One is apt to suppose that the woods about Birmingham must be blighted.' Still, despite the odd disappointment with the patterning on the china, it's not hard to imagine Jane making herself comfortable there; and to imagine how comfortable it might have been for thousands of similar households, in similar situations.

There is, though, something missing from this airily formal space: all the other people one had to share it with. As Jane wrote in 1801 before the move to Bath, 'We plan having a steady Cook, & a young giddy Housemaid, with a sedate middle aged Man, who is to undertake the double office of Husband to the former and sweetheart to the latter.' This basic trio, plus additions, would have been found in middle-class households all over the country, and there was indeed a similar housekeeping arrangement at the Rectory at Steventon – with the cook labouring at a range to feed both the Austen family and however many young students the Revd George Austen had taken on; that poor drudge, the housemaid, keeping the rooms clean, blacking the grates, serving the food, taking up hot water for washing, making the beds; and the Man doing battle with the garden and the fruit trees, or dealing with the general fabric of the house and its outbuildings. Once a week these numbers would have been swelled by a washerwoman who came in and laundered clothes and bed linen, often monopolizing the only freshwater tap (if you had one, rather than a pump in the courtyard) for the purpose. And depending on your location, a night-soil man – ghastly, but commonplace job – would appear and take away the contents of your outdoor privy, which might also contain the discarded contents of the chamber-pots stationed in every bedroom.

In other words, a reasonably modest establishment would have been routinely loud with human activity. There were the constant, shifting, intrusions of servants and other occupants; there were the arrivals and depart-ures of one's more distant family and family friends; there were passing callers and overnight visitors, all with their own business to transact, their own physical presences, their own habits of shouting and door-banging. Privacy, a sense of sovereign space in the middle of all this, would have been extremely hard to sustain. And, just to top it off, the home would have smelled, pretty powerfully – what with the cooking, the hard-to-keep-fresh fruit and vegetables, the coal-smoke, the unwashed clothing, the rarity of any serious bathing – and perhaps a touch of damp in the cellar. For all the nicety of address we respond to in Miss Austen's novels, this world was invasive, noisy, strongly scented, incon-venient, busy.

To find some peace, one had to go to a larger, or as Jane would put it, 'considerable' establishment.

Jane was no stranger to good living, although she would doubtless have been happy to have enjoyed more good living than she actually got. Writing to Cassandra from Godmersham in November 1813, she observed, snugly, 'I did not mean to eat, but Mr Johncock has brought in the tray, so I must. I am all alone. Edward is gone into his woods. At this present time I have five tables, eight-and-twenty chairs, and two fires all to myself.' And a few days later: 'I find many *douceurs* in being a sort of chaperon, for I am put on the sofa near the fire, and can drink as much wine as I like'. This mixture of comfort and spaciousness was just about the highest domestic state to which one could sensibly aspire: not surprising that it features so prominently in the novels.

Godmersham is still a seriously big house. Its central building is flanked by two imposing wings (one containing an orangery), it has a splendid entrance hall decorated with plasterwork fruit and flowers and an equally elegant drawing room in the style of William Kent, the walls hung with plaster musical instruments. No fewer than three walled gardens lie to the west of the main house, while an impressive eighteenth-century stables abuts the kitchen courtyard. In Miss Austen's day, it not only had all this, it had its own butler, Mr Johncock, which tells you most of what you need to know. Only the grandest establishments could run to a butler, whose existence would have indicated the presence also of a housekeeper, a cook, a head gardener and numerous maids and boys – a staff of anything between fifteen and twenty-five in total. Would Godmersham have made a good Pemberley? One body of opinion has it that Chatsworth, the Duke of Devonshire's near-palace in Derbyshire, is the inspiration for Pemberley; but if you weren't being greedy, then yes, it would.

Not that there wasn't an intervening layer of owner-
ship between Jane's relatively simple dwelling at Chawton and the finery of Godmersham. A prosperous farmer
– Robert Martin, in *Emma*, for instance – would have
lived in some comfort, in a substantial property, shared
(perhaps) with some of the unmarried farm-hands
(accommodated in the attic) but respectable nonetheless;
especially if, like Martin's, it had a 'Broad, neat gravel-
walk, which led between espalier apple-trees to the front
door'. Inside, such a home would have a sense of wider
possibilities about it, with a large kitchen, a dining-room
big enough for a family to congregate in, a parlour and
any other sitting-rooms or smaller spaces the farmer felt
like including. A dairy, a scullery, a brew house and a
bake house were also options – adding not only to the
substance of the place but contributing to its ease and
quality of living, with good food permanently on hand,
and much more generously available than an Austen-
sized home could have expected from its kitchen garden,
handful of chickens ('All alive and fit for the table, but
we save them for something grand') and one cow.

And yet, for all its comforts, such a place is not, as
Emma reveals, sufficiently aspirational. A 'considerable'
establishment would also have farms as its satellites, the
revenues and produce from which would partly or
wholly enable the owner of the big house to lead a
gentlemanly life. And if there wasn't farmland, there
were, as we learn of the Woodhouses, unnamed alternatives: 'The landed property of Hartfield certainly was
inconsiderable, being but a sort of notch in the Donwell
Abbey estate, to which all the rest of Highbury

belonged; but their fortune, from other sources, was such as to make them scarcely secondary to Donwell Abbey itself, in every other kind of consequence'. Money, at any rate, was what mattered; your status then depended on how tastefully or offensively you spent it.

How did you spend it? On improving the great house. After all, if you have money, and you've passed as much time as you feel able in hunting, shooting and visiting London, then you turn your attention to the property which defines you. You yearn, rightly or wrongly, to leave your mark on it. Godmersham dates from 1732, and has been built on ever since it first saw the light of day. Goodnestone Park, in Kent, is another eighteenth-century mansion familiar to Miss Austen: dating from 1704, it was considerably added to at the end of that century. When she saw it, it would have boasted several great reception rooms, a fine main staircase and a suite of three new rooms on the eastern side, designed by the famous Scottish architect, Robert Mylne. And there was the Vyne in Hampshire, a seventeenth-century house given a startling neo-Classical staircase in the late 1700s by its owner, John Chute, along with a pair of glamorous drawing rooms and a stone gallery. Vyne was also visited by Miss Austen, who would have had to admire its flashy additions.

And what went for the house, went for the grounds. This was the age of landscape designer Humphry Repton and the picturesque, the search for narrative excitement in the scene. Repton was ruthless in carving out vistas that set the house at the dramatic centre of the landscape, noting that 'Every sacrifice of large trees must be made with caution; at the same time, there may be situations in which trees are not to be respected for their size; on the contrary, it is that which makes them objectionable'. Less radical than renowned landscape architect Capability Brown, Repton nevertheless set a tone that made it almost impossible to look at one's estate and not be dissatisfied by some part of it. Follies and bald sweeps of grass – the Capability Brown look – were out; planting and terracing – the Repton style – were in.

For Jane Austen, though, there was something fatal about these modernizings. As it happens, both Darcy – 'The best landlord' – and Mr Knightley – who would 'Rather be at home, looking over William Larkins's week's account' than dancing – exemplars of virtue in the narrative scheme, are not only properly connected to the community at which they sit: they both have an aversion to improvement for its own sake.

Knightley's Donwell Abbey, 'Was just what it ought to be, and looked what it was ... the residence of a family of such true gentility, untainted in blood and understanding.' At the same time, it has an 'Abundance of timber in rows and avenues, which neither fashion nor extravagance had rooted up.' While Pemberley, as we know, is a paragon of discretion in the eyes of Elizabeth Bennet: 'She had never seen a place for which nature had done more, or where natural beauty had been so little counteracted by an awkward taste.' The point is driven home by the way the more unreliable characters in Austen's novels impose fashions on houses, mistaking modernity for taste, turning existing buildings around and tacking on unsuitable spaces and eye-catching features. Lady Catherine de Bourgh, a case in point, has installed a chimney-piece costing, according to Mr Collins, 'Eight hundred pound'. Henry Crawford determines that Edmund Bertram's house at Thornton Lacey 'Must be turned to front the east instead of the north – the entrance and principal rooms, I mean, must be on that side, where the view is really very pretty; I am sure it may be done. And *there* must be your approach, through what is at present the garden.' And Robert Ferrars is mad for cottages ('And that, I fancy, will be the end of it'). The great house, therefore, is more than a statement of wealth; it becomes a statement of virtue, in the right hands; a statement of impropriety in the wrong ones.

Having made the move from minor to major house, though, what happens next? In the very broadest sense, you carry on doing what you did before. When Jane went to Godmersham, she was given wine in smarter glassware than she would have used at Chawton, and she had her own personal maid (Sackree, who cost so much to tip). But she still had a fire lit in her room by a servant, played the piano, wrote letters, went for walks, paid visits, didn't do the cooking or washing-up and read by candlelight.

The lighting was a problem wherever you went. The farm labourer would have made do with tallow candles (a hempen or cotton wick dipped in animal fat) or rushlights (the pith of a rush, also dipped in animal fat) to provide a feeble, smoking, flame. The Austens and their like were better served than this, but only to a degree. Coal-gas lighting was a practical possibility by the early nineteenth century (in London, Pall Mall had been lit by gas in 1807, Westminster Bridge in 1813) but it was still a public, municipal, kind of light. So everyone else had to use candles made from relatively hard-to-obtain whale oil, or beeswax if they really wanted to impress. But they were expensive, not least because they were highly taxed. Even well-to-do households did their best to protect their candle stocks from decay and rats, re-using the stubs, and only occasionally using candles *en masse* to light an entire room. Instead, one tended to carry one's light around in a candlestick, a personal and specific source, whether one was in the cosy fastness of Chawton or the open spaces of Godmersham. 'We have got the second volume of *Espriella's Letters*,' Jane told Cassandra, 'and I read it aloud by candle-light': a typical sharing of the resource, and a reminder of how very gloomy the Regency could be once the sun went down.

Still, the big house had many compensations. It may have been gloomy, but when Jane sat down to dinner, she might have found herself in the company of as many as twelve other people, with silverware, fine Kings and Queens cutlery and many expensive candles set in candelabra of bronze, ormulu and marble. 'We had a very pleasant dinner,' she wrote from Godmersham, 'at the lower end of the table at least'. And when she went for a walk, she would never have needed to leave the grounds of the property, merely strolling around the park: at one time, Godmersham covered nearly 3,000 acres of prime Kentish land. Horses and carriages were kept permanently in the stables for journeys of any distance ('Yesterday passed quite *à la* Godmersham: the gentlemen rode about Edward's farm'). And reading or writing was, as Austen implies with her five tables and eight-and-twenty chairs, made extra-pleasurable by space, by the absence of crowds.

Perhaps that was the greatest luxury of the great house: room to move. 'I enjoy my apartment very much,' Jane declared during a stay in 1808, 'and always spend two or three hours in it after breakfast. The change from Brompton quarters' – where her brother Henry was, in London – 'to these is material as to space. I catch myself going on to the hall chamber now and then.' Space, as ever, was the great privilege, the great decider. Space; and the opportunity to look out of the window on a fine morning, and see, not ploughed fields, or a patch of grass, or a hedge, but acre upon fine acre, stretching away.

II. Dress

The one thing everyone knows about Jane Austen's Regency, is what the women looked like. The neoclassical influence – which found its way into architecture, painting, chinaware and furniture – had a surprisingly benign effect on women's fashion. The later decades of the eighteenth century are recognizable not least by the immensity and extravagance of women's dresses. Those vast skirts, nipped-in waists and expanses of bosom, which one recognizes from English painters Thomas Gainsborough and William Hogarth, were a clear provocation – especially when the wearers topped off the array with a hat half a yard across, or a Marie Antoinette-style coiffure, stuffed with feathers and fruit. A reaction was inevitable.

That reaction duly arrived in the form of the empire silhouette (with its nod to Napoleon) at the start of the nineteenth century. Introducing the extra-high, or even non-waistline, tucked right under the bust, the dress would fall away in a natural, flowing line, down to the ankle, or mid-calf. Muslin was the fabric of choice. This light, finely woven cotton material came originally from India, and made its first appearances in Europe in the seventeenth century. It was easy to keep clean; it kept its colour well when dyed; it could be patterned, embroidered, sprigged or painted; it looked particularly fetching in chic white and off-white; and it followed the shape of the wearer with just the right amount of becoming candour.

Jane, naturally, spends a good deal of time on the topic of muslin, both in the novels – as manifested by Henry Tilney and his good taste; or Harriet Smith, 'Hanging over muslins and changing her mind' at Ford's – and in her letters: 'I wore at the ball your favourite gown, a bit of muslin of the same round my head'; 'Bonnets of cambric muslin on the plan of Lady Bridges' are a good deal worn, and some of them are very pretty'; 'I was tempted by a pretty-coloured muslin, and bought ten yards of it on the chance of your liking it'; 'As I find the muslin is not so wide as it *used to be*, some contrivance may be necessary'; and so on. Velvet, silk and satin get much less coverage, literally, being used for ribbons and other decorative highlights; or to fit out the decor of a theatre. Lace, on the other hand, does feature more prominently, not least when Jane buys a black lace veil for the imposing sum of sixteen shillings.

That was the outer layer. The underpinnings had to be as stubborn as the exterior was refined – not least because the washerwoman, when she came to call, would attack underwear with a vengeance: items were routinely scrubbed with coarse soap in cold water, before being boiled. So drawers (which only arrived in the first decade of the nineteenth century) were made of stout cotton, linen or even wool fabrics. Chemises, or shifts – worn with or without drawers beneath – likewise had to be able to withstand serious washing, as their job was to soak up the wearer's dirt and sweat in order to protect the outer garments. Corsets, worn over the chemise, were a lot less onerous than eighteenth-century cinchers – slim young women could get away with not wearing a corset at all – but they too had to be extra-durable, with boning, reinforced cotton twill and a thing called a busk (a strip of wood to keep one's posture erect) down the front. Once all these things were in place, one or more cotton petticoats would be put on top, to give shape and opacity to the dress. It was a commonplace that muslin was quite transparent in certain lights, so the petticoat (often embroidered at the hem so as to make an additional display) had to provide modesty as well as extra warmth.

So far, so good. But what was the difference between morning dress (worn at home, for most of the day) and evening? If you were dressing for the evening, and you were a person of any pretentions at all, then your pretty sprigged muslin wouldn't be sufficient on its own. This was when all the beribbonings and trimmings had to be employed, along with a bolder colour scheme (pastels for the young ladies, authoritative blues, crimsons and purples for the more middle-aged), sumptuous embroidery, long gloves, bare shoulders and sometimes excessively bare bosoms. According to one authority, 'Although a few daring spirits, who went so far as to expose the breasts, were hissed in the street, the costume of the majority of women was not very much more prudish.' The simple cap favoured by Miss Austen for everyday wear would be replaced by, say, a satin turban, trimmed with ostrich feathers, courtesy of the *plumassier*; or the head would be left bare, the better to show off the hair, tightly curled at the brow with curling papers, and enlivened with ribbons and feathers. On the feet were incredibly frail pumps, like ballet slippers, made of soft kid or silk, and trimmed with a bow.

As for the face, well, the eighteenth century taste for very white faces and very red lips – achieved with appalling lead-based cosmetics – had given way to something much more natural in appearance. Etiquette guide *The Mirror of the Graces, or the English Lady's Costume* appeared in 1811, and provided this rebuke to an earlier taste: 'Nothing but selfish vanity, and falsehood of mind, could prevail on a woman to enamel her skin with white paints'. Bearing this in mind, cheeks were still judiciously lightened, but only with a dusting of powder (rice flour or talcum). Some rouge was also permissible, but nothing too elemental (a blusher, made of carmine or safflower) and perhaps some Rose Lip Salve, to heighten the colour of the mouth, without obliging the wearer to 'Lacker her lips with vermillion'.

But for outside wear? When Elizabeth Bennet tramps across the fields to reach her ailing sister, 'Jumping over stiles and springing over puddles with impatient activity', and 'Above her ancles in dirt', what was she wearing? We know that she ends up with 'Dirty stockings' and a 'Dirty petticoat'. We must assume that she was also wearing leather shoes, or, better, a pair of lace-up half-boots in leather or nankeen, rather than a pair of satin pumps. To keep out the rest of the elements she may have worn a cloak, a *pelisse* (a longish overcoat), a tailored redingote or maybe just a spencer (a short coat, ending at the waist). The whole would have been crowned – most likely – by a poke bonnet, that defining piece of clothing, pragmatically useful for keeping the rain and wind out; appropriately genteel, shuttering the wearer's face from vulgar inspection.

In fact the poke bonnet is emblematic of a whole style of dress: you only have to see one to extrapolate the rest of the outfit, seen on a hundred book jackets, observed in scores of Regency dramas. It also characterizes the relationship between stylishness and usefulness, the philosophical problem that animates fashion for both sexes. With women's fashions, one half-expects usefulness and fashionability to be on fairly poor terms – but at the start of the nineteenth century, men's fashions too, were convulsed. The arrival of men's fashion icon Beau Brummell and the cult of the dandy profoundly disrupted the connection between wearability and high style, pursuing a philosophy of extremes.

Most men – and certainly Jane Austen's men, even the Willoughbys and Crawfords – were perfectly sensible dressers, with their breeches or, increasingly, trousers, their dark topcoats (remembering Tom Lefroy's unfashionable light-coloured morning coat), plain white shirts and leather riding boots. A dark tall hat – an early topper – finished the ensemble. All the frills, the flashy embroidery, the powdered wigs and lace ruffles, the fopperies of an earlier generation had gone. Only the need for self-advertisement remained. Hence the startling success of George Bryan

Brummell. There was nothing inherently vulgar or ostenta-
tious about his philosophy of dress; in fact, it was quite in
keeping with the proprieties of the time. But it was an
extreme interpretation of those proprieties. Certainly, he
wore nothing louder than a dark blue topcoat (with brass
buttons), pale breeches, polished top boots and a stiff white
cravat. But his attention to detail went beyond perfection-
ism, revealing itself ultimately as obsessional behaviour of
the weirdest kind.

First things first: his keen interest in personal hygiene.
This area of human activity was, frankly, under-resourced
in 1800, with baths a prerogative of the well-to-do – who
could afford to have the water heated, brought to their
rooms and poured into a bath tub, but frequently never
bothered to do so – and everyone else making do with a
basin, a jug of water and a flannel, with which they might
give themselves a rub down. But Brummell declared
washing to be a cardinal virtue, and spent two hours every
day performing his ablutions. These involved not only
scrubbing himself with a fierce little brush and shaving with
a fastidiously tiny razor, but also plucking every unwanted
hair from his face with a pair of tweezers. His skin was
lobster-red by the end; but he was very clean, stylishly so
– and in this small way, managed to encourage the rest of
the gentlemanly class to start washing rather more than
they had hitherto been used to.

The same mania affected his relationship with his cravat.
Brummell's great invention was to use starched muslin in
order to create a fabulous meringue effect around the neck.
His immense white shirt collar then had to be folded down
to frame the cravat and hold it in place – a collar which was,

apparently, 'So large that, before being folded down, it completely hid his head and face, and the white neckcloth was at least a foot in height.' After that, it was a relatively simple matter to work the cravat down with the point of his chin so that he could see over it. And then, hours after he had started to dress, he could go out.

There were at least two by-products of Brummell's fixity of purpose. One was that, thanks in some measure to his insistence on the very highest standards from his tailors (one made his coat, another his waistcoat, a third his breeches) he helped raise the standard of all tailoring in London, gifting it a reputation which even the French respected. The second was found in the cult of the dandy: a group fixation that took the worst of Brummell's monomaniacal focus on physical appearance and ended up parodying it. London dandies, helpless in the face of their desperate need for recognition, were jeeringly known as 'Pinks of the Ton' and 'Veritable tulips'. One ageing society figure, looking back on the dandies' high noon, claimed that 'They were a motley crew with nothing remarkable about them but their insolence . . . and why they arrogated to themselves the right of setting up their own fancied superiority on a self-raised pedestal, and despising their betters, Heaven only knows.' The fact that their vanity was almost a kind of bravery – slashing their clothes with broken glass to denote lofty poverty; wearing 'Cossack' trousers, nipped in at the waist and ankles, with balloon legs in the middle – only made it more futile. And yet the cult persisted for years, fodder for the satirists and cartoonists, but still an expression of the need to perform, to seem special.

Back in Jane Austen's universe, where no dandy strayed, it meant this much: a respectable male character must be so respectable that his appearance is unremarked upon, except in the most general terms; and any suggestion of male vanity, whatever form it takes – Frank Churchill's haircut; Mr Elton's being 'A very pretty young man' – is an alarm bell ringing. Dressiness was strictly for the ladies.

III. Education and Accomplishments

It's hard not to feel some dismay at the way things were going for young women in the early 1800s. As the middle classes gradually swelled in number, and the life of the town increasingly infected the life of the countryside, so the idea of the useless woman – a pleasing adornment, rather than a competent individual with her own agenda – increasingly took hold. As one historian put it, 'It became a point of social pride that the young ladies should be taught by a governess in the schoolroom, and thence pass to the drawing-room, and do at all times as little domestic work as possible.' The imprisoning virtues of the Victorian age were gradually being fixed; for Jane, Cassandra and their like, there was only so much intellectual nurturing they could look forward to. In 1813, Jane actually described to Cassandra a trip she had made to a fashionable academy for girls in London: 'I was shewn upstairs into a drawing-room, where she' – Charlotte Craven, later Lady Pollen – 'came to me, and the appearance of the room, so totally unschool-like, amused me very much; it was full of modern elegancies, and if it had not been for some naked cupids over the mantlepiece, which must be a fine study for girls, one should never have smelt instruction.'

The two Austen girls had been packed off to a couple of ramshackle boarding schools in order to acquire the rudiments of gentility. Mrs Goddard's school, in *Emma*, sounds drawn from their experience, a place where 'A reasonable quantity of accomplishments were sold at a reasonable price, and where girls might be sent to be out of the way and scramble themselves into a little education, without any danger of coming back prodigies'. Jane once reminded her sister, 'I could die of laughter at it, as they used to say at school', suggesting a regime in which at least some laughing was done. But what else?

A generation earlier, a young woman would have had to know enough to be able to run the household – to read, write, keep accounts and have an idea of what managerial duties would be expected of her. But by the start of the nineteenth century, this basic list had acquired a different emphasis, an ambition for gentility and a shunning of practicality, with needlework, music, languages (the fashionable ones, Italian and French) all being promoted. And as the core subjects became more genteel, so it became increasingly important to be taught nicely at home, by a governess – a Jane Fairfax, rather than a Mrs Goddard. The young Jane Austen did indeed become adept at satin stitch: that decorative needlework which uses flat stitches to cover a section of the background fabric. 'I believe I must work a muslin cover in satin stitch to keep it from the dirt. I long to know what his colours are. I guess greens and purples', she wrote of a footstool worked by her nephew William. This industry with a needle and thread was perfectly proper. Overworked and underpaid seamstresses had a dreadful time of it, battling through their piecework; well-bred ladies could, however, spend as long as they liked on embroidering and adorning.

Music, too, was something you could commit yourself to, more or less without restraint, provided the results were bearable ('They will wish the twenty-four guineas in the shape of sheets and towels six months hence; and as to her playing, it never can be anything', Jane grumbled at the prospect of Anna Lefroy's parents buying her an expensive pianoforte), and the music teachers worth the candle ('They are all, at least music-masters, made of too much consequence and allowed to take too many liberties with their scholars' time'). In fact, you could scarcely have too much refinement of any sort – drawing, dancing, singing, playing – unless you were Bingley, in *Pride and Prejudice* and questioning the standards by which such skills were judged. 'I never heard,' he says, incredulously, 'a young lady spoken of for the first time, without being informed that she was very accomplished.' For him, and probably for many others, young women were reduced too easily to a collection of commonplace attainments, with a consequent devaluing of the currency of talent. For Jane, on the other hand, writing to Cassandra in 1811, 'Miss H. is an elegant, pleasing, pretty-looking girl, about nineteen, I suppose, or nineteen and a half, or nineteen and a quarter, with flowers in her head and music at her finger ends. She plays very well indeed. I have seldom heard anybody with more pleasure . . .'

At the same time, once formal schooling was over, it was possible for a young woman to feel acutely, or indistinctly, her own lack of education – if those two hotheads, Marianne Dashwood and Emma Woodhouse, are to be believed. Recovering from her illness in the latter stages of *Sense and Sensibility*, Marianne determines to 'Divide every moment between music and reading', and, 'By reading only six hours a-day, I shall gain in the course of a twelvemonth a great deal of instruction which I now feel myself to want'. While Emma, as Knightley reminds us, has always been engaged in a war with her own inattention: as evidenced by the list of book titles 'She drew up when only fourteen – I remember thinking it did her judgment so much credit, that I preserved it some time; and I dare say she may have made out a very good list now. But I have done with expecting any course of steady reading from Emma. She will never submit to any thing requiring industry and patience'. Jane Austen, skilled with a needle and thread, competent at the piano, and entirely comfortable with her own tastes in literature, was spared this sense of inadequacy. So far from feeling inadequate, of course, that she became the writer Jane Austen. She made herself more than competent, more than a woman of mere accomplishments. And as such, broke free of the surge towards uselessness which was threatening other, well-brought-up women; the Emmas and Mariannes of her novels.

Nor was she obliged to have anything to do with the grisly social nullity that was Almack's Assembly Rooms. For the really well-bred young woman, Almack's was a rite of passage that saw her finally dispatched into the world. Their premises were in King Street, off Piccadilly, in London. Membership cost ten guineas, and, according to a certain German nobleman, Prince Pückler-Muskau, what you found there was 'A large bare room, with a bad floor and ropes around it, like the horses' enclosure in an Arab camp; two or three equally bare rooms where the most wretched refreshments were served; and a company into which, despite the immense difficulty of getting tickets, a great many nobodies had forced their way.'

Still, it was here that the season's debutantes were shown off by their mothers, permitted to enjoy the staidest of dances (country dances, Scottish reels) with suitably unworrying young men, and generally put up for inspection. When there was a pause in the dancing, bread and butter, (allegedly) stale cake, lemonade, tea and, for the truly fortunate, ratafia – a very light liqueur, flavoured with fruit or almonds – were served. And then the process began again. It was known as 'The Marriage Mart'; and was run with boggling ruthlessness by a committee containing, among others, Lady Castlereagh, Princess Esterhazy, Lady Jersey, Princess Lieven and the daunting Mrs Drummond Burrell. Such was their grip that the Duke of Wellington was once turned away from the door for arriving slightly late; and for wearing trousers, rather than formal knee-breeches. Astonishingly, the Almack's ritual (also known as 'Hunt the Husband' and 'Debs for Sale') persisted well into the mid-nineteenth century; so long, in fact, that the young bloods who were obliged to turn up as dancing partners for the debutantes, worked out a post-Almack's routine, to preserve their sanity. They would leave King Street, make their way down to Smithfield and get plastered on 'blue ruin' – gin, in other words – in a boozer that became known as 'All-Max in the East'.

Which raises the question: what were the young men actually bringing to this party? What did they have to be so pleased about? What were *their* accomplishments?

In some ways, not much more than those of the young women. The nineteenth-century wholesale expansions of the English public school system were still some way in the distance, so the procedure for a son of the gentry was pretty well set. He would probably be sent to a tutor when young (a tutor such as George Austen, in fact) before being bundled off to board at Eton, Harrow, Winchester (where the Austen family was represented) or Westminster. At these monuments to all that was worst in human nature, bullying, sexual aggression, sadism and small-scale rioting were routine in the boys' lives. The masters often went in fear of their own charges, and the dormitories after dark were sinks of depravity. Greek and Latin were staples of the curriculum, with, unbelievably, many subjects – mathematics, algebra, modern languages – only available outside the normal schedule of lessons. At Harrow, mathematics wasn't compulsory until 1837, with English history and English literature being added some time after that.

In many ways, the great schools were not much more than exclusive penitentiaries, where boys could be sent to go through the nightmare of adolescence somewhere, anywhere, away from their parents. Henry Fielding called them 'The nurseries of all vice and immorality'; while H. H. Munro – rather later – epigrammatized it thus: 'You can't expect a boy to be vicious till he's been to a good school'. And the universities? They were more civilized, but scarcely more rigorous. The only two English Universities were Oxford and Cambridge (Scotland, with a reputation for higher educational standards, already had St Andrews, Glasgow, Aberdeen and Edinburgh) and the syllabus was in many ways a continuation of what little had been managed at school. Although an undergraduate had to keep terms – turn up, basically – little else was expected. So the time was spent, as seen with the fatuous John Thorpe, on pleasure: on horses, gaming, drinking – even prostitutes, who represented a considerable problem at Oxford around this time. As the historian Edward Gibbon wrote, a generation earlier, 'I spent fourteen months at Magdalen College; they proved the fourteen months the most idle and unprofitable of my life.'

And yet, somehow, young men were turned out into the world. George Austen got through his time at St John's, Oxford, without turning into a monster. We know that Mr Collins has been down the same path ('Though he belonged to one of the universities, he had merely kept the necessary terms') not least because clergymen had to attend university before they could be ordained. And we assume that upright characters such as Knightley, Darcy and Edmund Bertram have notionally been through the mix of tutor, public school and university. But after all that – where did a young man acquire his polish, attend to his learning, develop a degree of civility, especially when in the company of a young woman?

By picking up hints on the job, by observing others and by being something of an autodidact; by seeking out the company of like-minded souls. English writer William Cobbett would, some years later, produce his *Advice to Young Men* (1829) ('Pertinacity is a very bad thing in anybody, and especially in a young woman'; 'No youth, nor man, ought to be called your friend, who is addicted to indecent talk'; 'No girl ever liked a young man less for his having done things foolish and wild and ridiculous'); while

The Revd Edward Berens would knock out his *Advice to a Young Man Upon First Going to Oxford* (1832) ('Be on your guard against getting into the habit of telling long stories'). But these rambling codifications arrived just as the Regency was fading into history. It was down to the individual to make something of himself, much as it had been throughout the eighteenth century.

In a sense, a young Regency gentleman only needed a basic understanding of the world; he didn't *need* accomplishments in the way his sister might be deemed to, because his job was not to be attractive, but to deal with what his destiny held in store. And there were only so many destinies available to him: as the eldest son, he would expect to inherit whatever land or personalty his father left him; whereas a younger son would have to find some occupation – the Army or Navy, the Church, perhaps some mildly appropriate commercial enterprise (publishing, banking) – and do his best from there.

After which? For both parties, male and female, it was all about marriage and money: the start of a Jane Austen novel.

IV. The Day

Clearly, the nicest way for a youngish man to spend the waking part of his day, was to go hunting or riding, enjoy a fine evening meal and end up dancing or flirting with a young woman. The next best way was to pass the time dutifully about one's estate, with agents, stewards, factors, tenant farmers and account books – in the manner of a Knightley, or Sir Thomas Bertram on his return from Antigua – and play the part of the Squire. Failing that, life as a cleric was not to be despised, provided one was in possession of a decent living or livings.

The status of a country clergyman was generally high, and he would have access to both the ear and the dining-table of the Squire, or, as in the case of Mr Collins, of Lady Catherine de Bourgh. What the cleric actually *did* with his day was in many ways up to him: if he had enough money coming in from his livings, few dependants, possibly an inheritance from somewhere in his family, it might be enough for him just to emit a suitable note of pious gravity, leaving a hired curate to do the actual work of the Church. Since advowsons (the 'Right [in English law] of presentation to a benefice') were often dished out at the whim of the landowner who held them, someone with no interest in or experience of the priesthood might suddenly and unexpectedly find himself sitting on a very tidy sinecure. 'The offer of a liberal independent establishment is pleasing', wrote one lucky recipient; 'having now the idea of going into the church I thought it would be advisable to take a degree, or not, as might suit my convenience.' Livings could be sold at auction (Lord Egremont made a point of buying them up) and one advertisement made a point of mentioning the living's 'Extensive cover for game' as well as the 'Elegant and fashionable' society in the neighbourhood. A well-set-up Rector – a notch or two above the Revd George Austen – could thus live very pleasantly. His curate, on the other hand, might be scraping a dismal living on as little as £150 a year, trapped in a poverty as grinding and demoralizing as that experienced by his parishioners, and have all the work of marrying them, Christening them and, in due course, burying them.

This was at least less awful than being trapped at the bottom of the Armed Forces – where the life of a Naval Rating, in particular, was often genuinely excruciating, with rum, sodomy and the lash ('Of *Rears* and *Vices* I saw enough', as Mary Crawford smuttily jests) nothing less than everyday realities; and the sadism of some commanding officers more or less beyond belief. The superior Naval ranks led curiously bipolar existences, away from home for months at a time, sometimes seeing violent action, seizing enemy vessels and enriching themselves in the process; then finding themselves shelved on half-pay, housebound somewhere on the South Coast and practising their handicrafts – making knotted fringe (as did Frank Austen), or working on their carpentry (think of Captain Harville, in *Persuasion*). The two great advantages that the Navy held over the Army were that it was possible to rise through the ranks by personal endeavour (and some patronage, as in the case of William Price) and it was possible to make a fortune. Wentworth is an exemplar (a bit like Captain Jack Aubrey in Patrick O'Brian's *Master and Commander* novels) of the skipper who does well enough to retire on the proceeds. And, of course, Jane Austen, whose Naval brothers became Admirals, is always ready to give the Senior Service the benefit of the doubt. But the only Navy we see in her novels – in a way, the only Navy anyone would encounter, back in England – is one becalmed, on shore leave, getting by on half-pay.

The Army was rather different. Much more socially hidebound, it was the glamour service, provided you could get the right kind of commission. It required connections and real money to obtain a commission in the cavalry or the infantry: £1,000 to buy yourself an ensigncy in the Foot Guards; over £4,000 to make the rank of major in the cavalry. The uniforms alone cost a small fortune – but the effect on an impressionable young woman of, say, a Hussars' outfit (modelled on the Hungarian light cavalry of the fifteenth century), or a Guards' uniform, was beyond price. It was flashy, snobbish and Jane Austen is as cool on the Army as she is warm towards the Navy, allowing it only a subversive and destabilizing role in *Pride and Prejudice*. Typically, it is Wickham who joins the militia – a scratch force of lightly trained volunteers, readying themselves in case Napoleon invaded – for quite a lot less than it cost to get a commission in the regular Army, and, happily, as a way of deferring payment on his debts. The main employment of anyone in the militia, once they had struck camp in one town and pitched it in another, was to flirt outrageously with frivolous young women, and this Wickham and his colleagues duly do: in stark contrast to the sobrieties of Captains Harville and Benwick, in *Persuasion*.

Was there anything else, though, a well-brought-up young man might turn his hand to? The learned professions – especially medicine and the law – were still consolidating, still in the process of escaping the hinterland they currently occupied: somewhere better than a mere trade, but still too much like one to be tolerated by a person of any standing. Jane's own brothers reveal the limits of choice available to the gentry, with one brother becoming a clergyman, two joining the Navy, another becoming a member of the landed classes, and only Henry trying his hand at something different – publishing and banking – before reverting to type and likewise joining the clergy. In the Midlands, and the north of England, the Industrial Revolution was throwing up an entirely new class of inventor-entrepreneur; while London's merchant fraternity had been powerful for generations and would become even more powerful as time went on. Both of these social sub-groupings would in fact come to define the nineteenth century, forcing the old gentry to come to a new accommodation. But in 1815 (even allowing for the presence of someone like Mr Gardiner, in *Pride and Prejudice*) the old dispensations held.

And the women? It depends on where you start. The wife of a farmer or shopkeeper might spend her days managing the household, attending to domestic chores and, from time to time helping her husband with *his* work. The same might be said of Mrs Austen – dealing with a house full of children, a smallholding, and her overworked staff. Her genteel family connections were no great use in the daily running of the family and the management of servants and tradespeople. She had to do it herself, while the Revd George Austen struggled to bring in the money. And the same was doubtless true of the Naval households of Frank and Charles Austen, never quite as rich as they would like to be, muddling through as best they could.

A step up from this contemporary-looking environment of shared toil, of making ends meet, and we find ourselves in the world of the leisured gentry, the world of Jane Austen's novels. For a woman in this setting, work meant, in effect, society. Unless she was kept busy with her children, her job was to be social, or to enable others to be social.

This work could start as early as breakfast – bearing in mind that breakfast was likely to be a large-ish meal, taken at around ten o'clock in the morning – when visitors might need to be entertained (breaking a journey, or touring the neighbourhood). Then, calls were made. Jane's letters are, as one might expect, stiff with references to visits, undertaken and received: 'I am just now returned from Eggerton; Louisa and I walked together and found Miss Maria at home'; 'Harriot and Eliza dined here yesterday, and we walked back with them to tea'; 'Our cousin, Miss Payne, called in on Saturday'; 'We had a visit yesterday from Edwd. Knight, and Mr Mascall joined him here.' Much has been made of the Fifteen-Minute Rule, the convention that an unannounced call *had* to last a quarter of an hour, or risk causing offence. Equally, in both *Emma* and *Pride and Prejudice*, Austen turns the rule back on itself, by depicting characters formerly at ease with one another stay for fifteen minutes *and no longer*, precisely to indicate a new coolness in the relationship. The problems this created for the visitor – having to keep track of time in his or her head, while still thinking of something agreeable to say – were notorious; and it requires someone as distinguished and desirable as Mr Darcy to break the rule with decorum, when he stays 'Above half an hour' with Elizabeth Bennet.

However well or badly negotiated, these visits were a necessary currency, establishing associations and paving the way for longer encounters in the future. They could lead to gatherings at bigger meals than breakfast; invitations to balls; invitations to play games and make music. They also helped mediate between the self-actualizing world of men, and the more reactive world of women.

As did the constant flow of letters. These were part of a
closed network – sent from woman to woman, never from
a woman to a man, unless he was a family member or she
was already married to him, or at least, engaged (the
surreptitious correspondence between Jane Fairfax and
Frank Churchill is *just* made defensible by their secret
engagement). And the business of letter-writing was, like
visiting, industrious (twenty letters a day was not unknown) and rule-bound. It also depended on clear handwriting and reasonable eyesight. The need to keep one's
text to as few sheets of paper as possible – letters were paid
for by the recipient, not the sender; and were charged by
weight – required a degree of skill. So when Jane declared,
'I thank you for your long letter, which I will endeavour to
deserve by writing the rest of this as closely as possible',
and, 'Your close-written letter makes me quite ashamed of
my wide lines; you have sent me a great deal of matter', she
was not merely admiring Cassandra's facility with a pen,
but her admirable sense of economy in squeezing the most
words onto a sheet of paper. 'You are very amiable and very
clever to write such long letters,' she told Cassandra on
another occasion; 'every page of yours has more lines than
this, and every line more words than the average of mine. I
am quite ashamed.'

If, despite one's best efforts, the paper ran out but one
didn't want to impose the expense of an extra sheet on
the addressee, then the answer was to continue to write the
letter 'crossed' – that is, with a fresh text written over
the first, but set at right-angles, in order to stand a chance
of legibility. One character in the novels refers to the end
result as 'Chequer-work', which seems about right –

but really desperate correspondents would 're-cross', and set a fresh layer of writing at forty-five degrees to the second layer. Everything about letter-writing was, in short, a labour; a labour compounded by the emotional investment involved. After all, this was your one chance to communicate intimately with someone (very possibly) on the other side of the country; there were no alternatives, save a face-to-face encounter. Letters were freighted with expectations and obligations; and it was no wonder that so much time was spent starting them, adding to them, trying to encompass everything on that one sheet, working at the business of love and friendship.

V. Meals

Dinner is, in some ways, the point of the day to which everything tends: the cardinal moment, the big meal, at which anyone of any importance is going to be present, and after which entertainments of any significance can begin.

Luncheon didn't really exist in the early nineteenth century. Since breakfast came late, and dinner came early – anything from around half-past three in the afternoon for the country folk, to a provocatively fashionable half-past six in the evening, for Londoners – the midday meal tended to be no more than a snack. So the energies of the cook tended to be directed towards the end of the day.

The cook's energies were also bent on making the most of what ingredients one had – especially while the Napoleonic Wars ground on across The Channel. The chronic interruption of trade was a curse and an encouragement: it kept food prices high at the same time as it drove forward improvements in what was known as 'Scientific agriculture'. The great statistician, Sir John Sinclair, cried out, 'Let us subdue Finchley common; let us conquer Hounslow Heath; let us compel Epping Forest to submit to the yoke of improvement'. He was heeded and great efforts were made to increase the yields of grain and meat, all over the country. Nevertheless, in the latter stages of the war, a cow might fetch as much as £15 at auction, and a sheep £3, as prices crept up. At the same time, the Corn Law of 1804 kept bread prices high, with corn reaching well over 126 shillings a quarter in 1812 (falling to half that price three years later, when the war ended). Whatever one had, had to be used efficiently. Especially if you happened to be wretched poor, and forced to subsist on a diet of potatoes, occasionally brightened by a bit of bacon or cheese. A semi-skilled worker, earning perhaps fifteen shillings a week, might allow himself more expensive items, once in a while: tea, sugar, some fresh meat. But for the labourer, bread was generally out of the question, since a single loaf cost about the same as twenty pounds of potatoes.

Among the middling classes, a mixture of indulgence and prudence prevailed. In the Austens' Hampshire and Kent, they were generally fortunate with harvests and yields, and there was rarely anything that might be called *want*. On the other hand, there was never much money in the Austen house, so offers of fruit and meat were always acceptable, and what was in store had to be used wisely. Jane's letters are full of hungry references to meals and to foodstuffs: we find gooseberries, mutton, currants, pheasant, spare ribs, lobster, honey, apples, butter, tea (a tremendous number of references to tea), venison, cheesecake, mustard and 'Fourteen bottles of mead'. Sometimes the food is for her own consumption (the black butter of Portsmouth, actually an apple preserve, no butter involved, is 'Neither solid nor entirely sweet'); sometimes it is for another member of the family (of a pig for one of her brothers: 'My mother means to pay herself for the salt and the trouble of ordering it to be cured by the sparibs, the souse, and the lard'). Whichever it is, she is conscientious in her reports on it ('A most comfortable dinner of soup, fish, bouillée, partridges, and an apple tart'; 'Venison quite right'; 'My father's mutton, which they all think the finest that was ever ate'); and on its effects ('Composition seems to me impossible with a head full of joints of mutton and doses of rhubarb').

The combination of a broadening middle class plus a need to be careful with food, could only mean one thing: the first cookbooks began to appear. Hannah Glasse's *The Art of Cookery Made Plain and Easy* (1747) was already in print; while Eliza Acton was beginning to contemplate her *Carefully Tested Recipts*, wondering how to combine frugality with sufficient luxury to make an entire book of recipes seem tempting. Her *Modern Cookery for Private Families* (first published in 1845), conceived at a time of high prices and occasionally uncertain supply, contains useful instruction about using up leftovers in sausage or paste form, as well as advice on the preparation of a cheap, nutritious but essentially hideous, calf's head; at the same time as it takes pheasants' breasts and swan's eggs more or less for granted. Variety was the thing. Despite the problems caused by the war, the English were widely held (even by the French) to eat well. Meals could quite plausibly range from skate with oyster sauce, followed by a knuckle of veal, some lamb, a plate of asparagus, some lobster and some raspberry tarts; to a more modest, but still satisfying repast, as envisaged by English writer William Hazlitt at the end of a day's walking – 'Eggs and a rasher, a rabbit smothered in onions, or a veal-cutlet'.

At the top end of consumption, of course, things were more elaborate. A relatively middle-class dinner would be expected to offer at least a reasonably comprehensive selection of roasts and side dishes for the first course, followed by an equally substantial second course consisting of game, fish, vegetables and sweet dishes, with a special dessert, ordered from a confectioner's. But a grand society hostess would provide fifteen courses at least for her guests. Continental visitors were often boggled by the sheer amount and variety of food on offer, but griped by English attempts at haute cuisine – one noting that 'The French, or side dishes, consisted of very mild, but very abortive, attempts at Continental cooking, and I have always observed that they met with the neglect and contempt they merited'. Not that this could be said of meals served by and for the Prince Regent: a glutton of international standing, some of his banquets were so scandalously over-catered-for that at least one dinner included more than a hundred hot dishes – starting with turbot in lobster sauce, working its way through veal, pheasant, truffles, apricots and oysters, and staggering to a halt with a chocolate soufflé.

Miss Austen, much like the rest of the population, never came near such superabundance; but even she found that there were times when there was more food on the table than anyone could cope with. 'We could not with the utmost exertion consume above the twentieth part of the beef', she wrote on one occasion; on another, to Cassandra, staying with brother Henry in London, 'You will have a turkey from Steventon while you are there, and pray note down how many full courses of exquisite dishes M. Halavant' – the chef – 'converts it into'.

And this is without even mentioning supper: a light meal taken at the end of the day, to steady oneself before retiring to bed – a rarebit perhaps, or a slice of pie. A supper, taken at half-past ten at night, may well be compensation for an hour 'Spent in yawning and shivering in a wide circle round the fire', while a dull guest failed to go home.

Then there was drink: as much as possible, whenever possible. Given that so little of the early nineteenth century's water was directly potable, least of all in towns and cities, it was a matter of simple necessity to drink something that contained boiled water – beer or tea – or which was made from grapes. This meant that the working man lived pretty much on beer, while the better-off would take wine as often as possible. Willoughby's pint of porter on his way to Marianne's sick bed is a pretty modest indulgence ('I am very drunk,' he says, mockingly), even though today's conception of porter is of a dense, treacly beer, with a fairly high alcohol content. For him, it would have been about as eventful as a cup of coffee.

The presumption was that a gentleman – a Darcy, a Knightley – lived by alcohol. Pitt the Younger was famous for his ability to get through six bottles of port a day and remain functional, and one or two heroically constituted drinkers were believed to manage twice that much. Yes, the bottles were smaller than today's – nearer half a litre than three-quarters – and the alcohol content of Regency era port was lower; more like that of a modern table-wine. But the quantities were still prodigious. Breakfast for even a relatively self-denying drinker might be accompanied by claret or ale, or perhaps a hock and seltzer to settle the stomach. A glass of sherry or Madeira was taken in the middle of the morning, any outdoor activities would require a brandy bottle along the way, and then, by five in the evening, the champagne would come out. And that would be followed by other types of wine, port, brandy and possibly more champagne to round off the day.

French wines (other than champagne) were often frowned upon as being insufficiently hefty for the determined English drinker – quite apart from being increasingly difficult to come by as the war with France dragged on and the stuff had to be smuggled across the Channel. Iberian wines – port, Madeira, sherry – were much more to the nation's robust tastes. Anything decent, French or otherwise, was expensive – Madeira costing seven guineas for a dozen bottles, champagne eleven guineas per dozen, port, around five pounds. This costliness was partly (but only partly) responsible for the conceit that a gentleman should show his indifference to financial caution by spending the whole day borderline drunk. When John Thorpe describes how at the last party he threw in Oxford 'Upon average we cleared about five pints a head', he is therefore merely being true to form.

Drinking activity wasn't confined to men. We know that Miss Austen was quite comfortable with the idea that she could be put next to the fire at Godmersham and be left to drink as much wine as she liked; and that when she intended to 'Eat ice and drink French wine, and be above vulgar economy', she was genuinely looking forward to it. Nevertheless, beverages such as ratafia and orange wine were invariably retained for the less confident female drinker – as was *the* drink of the day: tea.

China tea had been available since the end of the seventeenth century, luring enthusiasts away from coffee and chocolate despite its comparative rarity and expense. By the time of the Regency, a pound of tea cost anything from two and sixpence to twenty shillings a pound, and was being carefully preserved – often in lockable caddies, alongside the similarly costly sugar. Inevitably, Jane Austen's letters are punctuated with references to tea, either as the name given to the relatively informal mid-afternoon encounter, or the drink. 'We began our China tea three days ago,' she wrote in 1811, 'and *I* find it very good.' Later, she asks Cassandra to 'Let me know when you begin the new tea, and the new white wine. My present elegancies have not yet made me indifferent to such matters.' And some time after that, she finds herself contemplating a long-standing problem: 'I am sorry to hear that there has been a rise in tea. I do not mean to pay Twining till later in the day, when we may order a fresh supply.' And here, she touches on a larger issue.

The price of tea would remain high for years: so a minor industry grew up, adulterating the product and selling it on to a keen and unquestioning public. China tea was fairly easy to fake, using thorn leaves, which were painted with (poisonous) verdigris – copper carbonate – and added in quantity to the real thing. Indian tea was rather harder to simulate, but it could be done with a horrible mixture of used tea leaves (acquired from kitchens and taverns), gum and (poisonous) black lead. Since the Austens were getting their tea from the very proper firm of Twinings, it's likely that they went unharmed. Others, though, didn't. In fact, drinks of all sorts were peculiarly vulnerable to adulteration, and the poorer you were, the more likely you were to be on the receiving end of some kind of vile fraudulence. Gin, although no longer the scourge of the working-classes that it was in the mid-eighteenth century, was still being made with sulphuric acid and turpentine; while beer was stiffened and flavoured with anything from green vitriol and picrotoxin (a poisonous plant compound), to bitterwood, liquorice, treacle and tobacco. 'Old port' was artificially generated by adding super-tartrate of potash; wines routinely acquired a nuttier flavour thanks to bitter almonds, which contained prussic acid; milk was frothed up by having snails stirred into it.

It was, of course, easier to fix up a drink, rather than a solid foodstuff. There was only so much you could do to a piece of bacon, or a fish, before it became obvious that something was wrong with it. This didn't stop other foods from getting the treatment, though. Bread was bulked out with alum; pickles were given a lively green colour by the addition of copper; boiled sweets were made more appealing to children by introducing salts of copper and lead; the orange rind of Gloucester cheese came from red lead. The rudiments of public health legislation (such as the Gin Act of 1751) were only just being contemplated, and it was easy to get away with the most horrible botchings. For Jane, who usually lived close to the source of production, freshness and reliability were less of a worry. The moment she went to Bath or London, however, she was potentially in the grip of sharp practice, however much Henry's money might have insulated her from the worst of it. 'In London it is always a sickly season,' Mr Woodhouse sighs, in *Emma*; 'Nobody is healthy in London, nobody can be'. He was thinking, specifically, of the air; but the cheese on one's plate had to be treated with caution, too.

VI. Pleasure

Once dinner was over, and assuming that no one was ill with lead poisoning, the ladies retired to the drawing-room, leaving the men to finish off the wine and then make their way (singly or collectively, there was no general exodus, as in the Victorian era) to join them. What next? Some sort of entertainment.

For this, one could go out, or one could stay in. Going out (and this would mean a relatively modest dinner) could mean a trip to another private house; or to the Assembly Rooms, perhaps. It would also mean, in all probability, going on or near a night when there was a full moon, in order to make the journey more comfortable, and less likely to be interrupted by footpads. Sir John Dashwood, of *Sense and Sensibility*, at one point tries to get an impromptu party together for the evening, 'But it was moonlight and every body was full of engagements'.

If one stayed in – or indeed, if one was joined by others coming from elsewhere – then various options were available. Arguably the most innocuous way to spend the time was in solving 'Enigmas, charades or conundrums', such as those Jane Austen played with her young nephews. These fascinate Emma Woodhouse to the extent of her 'Collecting and transcribing all the riddles of every sort that she could meet with, into a thin quarto of hot-pressed paper'. That said, Emma corrupts their essential harmlessness by using them to tease and entangle Harriet Smith, dragging Mr Elton into the business at the same time; and again, later on at Box Hill, as an unintended opportunity to insult Miss Bates. Which actually means that – open-ended and difficult to police – riddles and charades could lead to explorations of human nature which the reticent player might well not enjoy.

Card games were a more solid proposition. Indeed, they were a central component of just about any social evening, even though they entailed a tiny amount of gambling. Since it was possible for London gamesters to lose thousands of pounds at a game as harmless as whist, respectable company played for the smallest stakes imaginable. But they did have a decent range of games to choose from: cassino, loo, quadrille, piquet, commerce, brag, speculation, whist and vingt-un could all be played in the most cautious society. Cassino was a pickup game, in which open cards on the table were used to make number combinations; piquet was a trick-taking game with complications; speculation was a (mock) gambling game, with tokens for money, the holder of the highest trump card taking the pot; loo also involved gambling tokens, with players betting on how many tricks they thought they could take; quadrille was a trick-taking game related to whist; commerce involved making card combinations; vingt-un was a forefather of pontoon. Different degrees of skill and devilry were required by each game, but Jane's favourite was speculation. She compared it unfavourably with brag, demanding to know 'What is there so delightful in a pair royal of Braggers? It is but three nines or three knaves, or a mixture of them. When one comes to reason upon it, it cannot stand its ground against Speculation'; before composing a little poem on the subject:

Alas! poor Brag, thou boastful game!
What now avails thine empty name?
Where now thy more distinguished fame?
My day is o'er, and thine the same,
For thou, like me, art thrown aside
At Godmersham, this Christmas tide;
And now across the table wide
Each game save brag or spec. is tried.
Such is the mild ejaculation
Of tender-hearted speculation.

Commerce, on the other hand, made her uneasy, not least because of the expense. While staying at Portsmouth, she found herself drawn into 'A second pool of commerce,' one evening, which 'was the ruin of us; it completed the prosperity of Mr Debary, however, for he won them both'. A week later:

We found ourselves tricked into a thorough party at Mrs Maitland's, a quadrille and a commerce table, and music in the other room. There were two pools at commerce, but I would not play more than one, for the stake was three shillings, and I cannot afford to lose that twice in an evening.

But if anything could be said to be essential to the success of an evening, it was cards. And card games punctuate the novels as inevitably as they punctuated life – whether speculation, in the Parsonage at *Mansfield Park* ('Lady Bertram bids a dozen for that queen; no, no, a dozen is more than it is worth. Lady Bertram does not bid a dozen. She will have nothing to say to it'); commerce, at Mr Thorpe's house, in *Northanger Abbey* (or else in the card-room of the Upper Rooms at Bath); or in the drawing-room at Netherfield, in *Pride and Prejudice*, where Elizabeth Bennet 'Found the whole party at loo, and was immediately invited to join them; but suspecting them to be playing high, she declined it'.

And yet, for all its intrigue and mental stimulation, there was one thing a game of cards could not supply. When one had exhausted all the possibilities of conversation, and one had taken one's tea, and one had had one's fill of organized games, and one had made all one's wagers, what was the very best thing one could do? Dance. Because dancing, by definition, was best done with a member of the opposite sex.

Dancing could take place on a small scale, a dance at home, with someone playing the piano and no more than five couples capering around a room with the furniture pushed back. Otherwise it could be done on the grand scale, at the Upper Assembly Rooms in Bath, with an orchestra, a Master of Ceremonies and jostling crowds. At the height of its popularity towards the end of the eighteenth century, the ballroom of the Upper Rooms would find itself home to as many as eight hundred dancers, all contained in a space one hundred feet long by forty-odd feet wide. Beau Nash, the first and greatest Master of Ceremonies, wrote a rule-book in the mid-eighteenth century governing behaviour at such huge events. This was adopted in Assembly Rooms all over the country, and formed the basis for subsequent Upper Rooms rule-books. One such book, dating from the end of the Napoleonic Wars, required balls to start at eight in the evening, to have the rooms 'Regularly and properly' lit a quarter of an hour beforehand and to be finished 'At half-past eleven o'clock precisely, except on the night of the King's Birthday and on the nights of the two balls given for the Master of Ceremonies when the time of dancing shall be unlimited.' The Austens may have submitted to an earlier, stricter, ordinance, which saw the dancing begin at six p.m., with minuets only for the first two hours, followed by country dances at eight, tea at nine and an end by eleven o'clock – but the structure was the same. There were also rules concerning the seating arrangements for 'Ladies of precedence', the strict prohibition of 'Trowsers or colored pantaloons' and the right of ladies 'To be considered perfectly free in regard to accepting or declining partners'. For the 1811–12 season at Bath, a subscription to twenty-four Monday night balls cost twenty-six shillings. This entitled the subscriber to admission on each ball night, plus two extra tickets *'Transferable to Ladies only'*. There was an additional charge of sixpence on admission for tea; while a ticket bought at the door cost five shillings.

Once the ball was under way, the Master of Ceremonies' job included the vital functions of making sure the ball was opened by the most important lady present and introducing appropriate young men as dancing partners for young women. This we see happen with Henry Tilney ('A very gentlemanlike young man') and Catherine Morland at the start of *Northanger Abbey*. After that, it was pretty much a free-for-all, with men asking women to dance as their inclinations bade them – the proviso being that you were only allowed two dances in succession with any one partner before you had to move on. The same rules applied at smaller functions, except that there was no need for a Master of Ceremonies. To have hundreds of dancers in the Upper Rooms at Bath was a rarity ('There was only one dance, danced by four couple', said Jane, grieving), and unknown anywhere else. The Assembly Rooms at Basingstoke were doing well to have twenty couples dancing at any time, and a private party could get by with just five. When the twenty-year-old Jane Austen actually opened the dancing at Goodnestone one evening, there were four couples, and one piano.

Not that this is sufficient for Frank Churchill in *Emma*, who argues, while plotting a dance at Randalls, his father's house, that 'Five couple are not enough to make it worth while to stand up', and agitates instead for ten. To this Emma replies that 'It would be dreadful to be standing so close! Nothing can be farther from pleasure than to be dancing in a crowd – and a crowd in a little room!' Given that there would probably be only one musician making the music (such as the solitary fiddler referred to in *Mansfield Park*), anything much above ten couples would be too noisy for any player to make himself heard – to say nothing of the racket generated by all the other, non-dancing guests.

Whether the event was big or small, the most popular dances were, for many years, country-dances – a corruption of *contre-danse*, itself a variation of an earlier kind of English dance in which dancers faced one another, and as many as eight couples engaged in the same formation. For many young men and women, this was the nearest they would get (outside a formal betrothal) to any kind of reciprocated intimacy, so it was important to seize the opportunity. Jane's sad reflection, written from Portsmouth in 1808 – 'The melancholy part was, to see so many dozen young women standing by without partners', a circumstance brought about by the numbers of men who had gone off to deal with the French threat – was gloomy enough for her, but bordering on the tragic for the younger women who had come in search of romance. In happier times, the only drawback was that one had to dance with every other partner, in the manner of Scottish reeling, say, before working one's way back to the person one was especially interested in. This process could take as long as thirty minutes ('It would look odd to be entirely silent for half an hour together', Elizabeth Bennet points out to Darcy), as everyone worked their way through dance tunes such as the 'Trip to Tunbridge' or the 'Bath Assembly'.

The square-formation cotillion was a dance of Jane Austen's youth; at the end of her life, the quadrille, another square-formation dance, was becoming fashionable: 'Much obliged for the quadrilles, which I am grown to think pretty enough, though of course they are very inferior to the cotillions of my own day', she wrote to Fanny Knight in 1816. More problematic was the waltz, which was very new and far too sexy. Instead of enjoying the shared gentilities of formation dancing, with the waltz one found oneself suddenly in close proximity to one partner and one partner only, for as long as the music lasted. Princess Lieven, of the stuffy Almack's, had given the dance a veneer of respectability by dancing it with Lord Palmerston (who served twice as Prime Minister); but even Lord Byron was shocked when it first came across to England from the Continent – calling it both 'seductive' and 'voluptuous'.

Waltzing was not, fortunately, a problem that Miss Austen had to deal with. Provided that dancing, with all its opportunities for sexual tension and inner confusion, makes an appearance in her stories, she is content: *Sense and Sensibility*, *Pride and Prejudice*, *Mansfield Park*, *Emma* and *Northanger Abbey* are all dance-friendly; only *Persuasion* refuses to make much of it, using it instead as an index of Anne Elliot's marginalization, keeping her forever in the background, 'Very much preferring the office of musician to a more active post'. Dancing, and the hinterland which went with it, were, in some ways, the highest social activity to which any society might aspire. But one had – unlike Anne Elliot – to aspire in the first instance.

VII. Manners

Modern readers cannot help but notice that the manners of Jane Austen's characters are a good deal more formal than those we are currently used to. Extremely diligent modern readers may even have noticed one or two discrepancies in etiquette between the earlier novels and the later ones. And some readers may have got no further than a state of hopeless confusion in trying to understand the conventions behind naming young, unmarried, women. How do we sort this out?

Names first. When there are several sisters – as with *Sense and Sensibility*, *Pride and Prejudice* – the eldest is properly referred to by her surname. Elinor Dashwood is 'Miss Dashwood'; Jane Bennet is 'Miss Bennet'. Elizabeth Bennet, on the other hand, can be straightforward 'Elizabeth', when referred to be the author; 'Miss Elizabeth Bennet', or 'Miss Elizabeth', when properly addressed by another character; 'Miss Eliza', informally but acceptably addressed by Sir William Lucas, an old family friend; 'Miss Eliza', informally and presumptuously addressed by Miss Bingley; 'Eliza', affectionately named by her confidante Charlotte Lucas (who is of course referred to as 'Miss Lucas' in the narrative); 'Lizzy', by her parents and her sisters.

Mr Darcy is naturally enough, 'Mr Darcy' – unless to his friend, Bingley, who is at liberty to refer to him merely as 'Darcy'. And, he is, often enough, known merely as 'Darcy' in the narrative: a liberty Miss Austen doesn't permit herself in *Emma*, where Mr Knightley is invariably 'Mr Knightley', except when treated with undue familiarity by Mrs Elton ('How can she find any appellation for them, deep enough in familiar vulgarity? She calls you, Knightley', cries an appalled Emma). Mr Darcy will, in theory, remain 'Mr Darcy' so far as Elizabeth Bennet is concerned, even when she has become Mrs Darcy; as Mr Bennet is inevitably 'Mr Bennet' to *his* wife. Darcy does go as far as calling Miss Elizabeth, 'Elizabeth' right at the end of the book, an indication of the depth of his feelings, just as Mr Knightley lovingly calls Emma, 'Emma', once circumstances allow. One of the sweetest exchanges in *Emma* arises when Emma declines to call Mr Knightley 'George' in return, insisting on 'Mr Knightley' in perpetuity: 'I will not promise even to equal the elegant terseness of Mrs Elton, by calling you Mr K.' Only at the altar, we are allowed to believe, will she go so far as to use his given name.

And these are just the forms of address. Everything else, too, has to follow a set of hierarchical conventions that to today's readers may evoke the complex codes of etiquette one associates with cultures of the Far East, but which were taken for granted by Miss Jane Austen and her readership at the time. A case in point: Mr Collins, as a clergyman, is axiomatically due a degree of respect from most of the rest of society; on the other hand, he oversteps the mark intolerably ('An impertinent freedom'), when he introduces himself to Mr Darcy. 'It must belong to Mr Darcy, the superior in consequence, to begin the acquaintance', we are reminded. But no, off he goes, causing Mr Darcy to eye him 'With unrestrained wonder', and, shortly after, with 'contempt'.

And this is just one moment – there are countless other hurdles to be surmounted. And even if the correct forms *are* observed, they mean nothing without a foundation of decency and sincerity. 'Their acquaintance soon promised as early an intimacy as good manners would warrant', we are told of the Crawfords, early on in *Mansfield Park*; but we learn soon enough that mere observance will not do, and that Sir Thomas Bertram, having directed his attention solely 'To the understanding and manners, not the disposition' – to intellect and deportment, in other words, but not to inner virtues – has failed, radically.

Which prompts one to wonder how anyone ever managed to engage romantically with the opposite sex. For those at the very bottom of society, there was often sufficient lack of supervision and/or lack of concern, to make casual sexual encounters possible. At the very top, from the Prince Regent down, mistresses were commonplace, infidelities and adulteries more so, with prostitution – from the 'Straw-chippers' and 'Nob-thatchers' of the London streets, to the smartest courtesans, such as the legendary Hariette Wilson – a fact of life. It's true that unease at so much sexual licence was starting to grow, as the libertinism of the eighteenth century gave way to the buttoned-up hypocrisy of the nineteenth; and it was also true that an unmarried young woman of good breeding was to be treated with respect. Other than that, however, it was pretty much open season.

But Jane Austen's polite society had none of these options available to them – and if they did decide to embrace the immoral, come what may (Lydia Bennet and Wickham; Willoughby and Little Eliza; Maria Bertram and Henry Crawford), then they were made to suffer. It *was* possible to enjoy time exclusively in the company of one other person of the opposite sex: carriages were shared, walks were taken, interviews took place in private rooms, without the world coming to an end. Miss Austen herself went off, aged twenty-five and completely unmarried, alone in a Phaeton & Four carriage with the notorious Mr Evelyn of Bath. But the clear presumption was that this sort of thing could only happen very infrequently. The rest of the time, one was seen to share the object of one's attentions with whoever else was in the room, or on the walk, or in the carriage.

The good news was that, given a reasonably spacious sense of time, perhaps a reasonably large room containing plenty of other people – with music and dancing to provide extra cover – it was possible to get to know the other party tolerably well. Lydia Bennet and her soldier-loving friends may have gone further than that; but Elizabeth and Darcy manage with a mixture of intuition and confrontation, and they do it with propriety. Does it matter that all they know of each other is what we – the literary chaperons – see in the novel? They at least enjoy the luxury of romantic love – not an option for Charlotte Lucas or Marianne Dashwood, whose marriages, we presume, are destined to succeed on their own, reduced, terms. Only Admiral and Mrs Croft, enjoying Jane Austen's special Naval dispensation, seem truly bound up in each other after years of marriage. For everyone else, married life – especially with children – is pragmatic, full of compromises and lived with a certain distance between the people involved.

VIII. Travel

For someone of Jane Austen's class, travel was central to a civilized life. Family visits took up a good deal of one's energies (Cassandra seems to have spent more time away from her various homes than actually living in them). Bath, which started off as a travel destination for the Austens, turned into their place of residence. Bath, though, was not only stuffy in character – with its Abbey, its 8 a.m. ritual taking of the waters, its formal dancing – but lacked the latest attraction to make it a truly desirable travel destination: the sea.

Sea-bathing had been on the agenda since the rise of the North Sea coastal town of Scarborough, early in the eighteenth century. Despite the cold of Yorkshire and the inhospitable North Sea, this spa town had capitalized handsomely on the apparently medicinal virtues of sea-water, and was now setting a pattern for all other seaside resorts. There was no real pleasure in sea-bathing, even though it was clearly more wholesome than bathing in the hot springs at Bath, where the scrofulous and the pustular sat in the same waters as the clean and healthy. No, sea-bathing was a course of treatment: Dr Russell, a frighteningly inventive Brighton physician, held that sea-water was a sovereign remedy for rheumatism, madness, rabies and 'Fluxions of redundant tumours'; and should be bathed in, drunk neat and combined with crab's eyes, snails, tar, 'Prepared wood lice' and milk. Sea bathing therefore had to be done under medical supervision, from a bathing-machine (which was pulled into the water by a horse) and in the privacy of a hooded enclosure. And it was done in winter, first thing in the morning. It was an ordeal.

What made it at all bearable was the belief that it was doing one good. It offered a refreshing mix of the virtuous and the self-gratifying, and what worked for Scarborough was soon found to work on the South Coast of England, at Weymouth, Sidmouth and Lyme Regis. George III first visited Weymouth in 1789. He went back thirteen times – and even sea-bathed there – confirming its importance as a destination of quality. Lyme, on the other hand, had a more rugged appeal: it was principally a working port, whose traffic was slowly disappearing as the ships got too big to use the harbour. But it enjoyed a picturesque location, as well as a dramatic man-made focal point in the form of the Cobb – the mighty harbour wall projecting into Lyme Bay.

Lyme clearly made an impression on Jane Austen when she visited it in 1803, and again in 1804. When the action of

Persuasion moves to Lyme, it invokes an uncharacteristic hymn of praise: 'A very strange stranger it must be, who does not see charms in the immediate environs of Lyme, to make him wish to know it better', says the authorial voice – quite unlike Miss Austen's usual practice – before going on to praise neighbouring Charmouth (with its 'Sweet, retired bay, backed by dark cliffs') and Pinny ('Where a scene so wonderful and lovely is exhibited, as may more than equal any of the resembling scenes of the far-famed Isle of Wight'). Jane's letter to Cassandra of September 1804, conversely, is rather more matter-of-fact, grumbling about the lodgings she and her parents have taken ('Nothing certainly can exceed the inconvenience of the offices, except the general dirtiness of the house & furniture & all its inhabitants'), remarking on a 'A new odd-looking man who had been eyeing me for some time' at the ball, and noting that a Miss Armstrong 'Seems to like people rather too easily'. The usual Austen mixture of asperity and self-deprecation, in other words – only changing tack in a 'P.S.' at the end, where she announces, startlingly, that 'The bathing was so delightful this morning & Molly so pressing with me to enjoy myself that I believe I staid in rather too long, as since the middle of the day I have felt unreasonably tired.' Such, though, was the potential for magic in the encounter: and whether it was Scarborough, Lyme, Sidmouth, Weymouth or Brighton, the seaside resort promised a new and wonderful experience.

It was Brighton, though, which came to monopolize the popular imagination. It's easy to assume that Brighton only became Brighton through the good offices of the Prince Regent. But it had been consolidating its reputation as a fashionable resort on the south coast of England since the middle of the eighteenth century. The Duke of Marlborough frequented it, as did Fanny Burney and the Duke of Cumberland. The smart set began to appear in order to get healthy, and the town obliged the smart set by dedicating itself increasingly to pleasure. Towards the end of the eighteenth century, as one journal put it, 'The pretty women all hasten to see the Paris of the day.' The persistent Francophilia of the English upper-classes – their chronic desire to be among the French – never really left them, not even when war was being waged against the tyrant Bonaparte, and travel to the Continent became very difficult. But if the real Paris was off-limits, Brighton at least now presented itself as a louche new alternative destination, capable of moderating some of the disappointment.

Brighton offered two sets of Assembly Rooms, each offering the favoured trio of ballroom, supper room and card room, all tricked out with columns and friezes, and promoting card parties, Promenades and Public Teas. There was a proper Master of Ceremonies to effect introductions and keep the riff-raff out – so efficiently that, according to a contemporary, he 'Became Dictator, he promulgated laws, and all willingly yielded obedience'. There were plays, there were two libraries (which provided useful cover for illicit encounters), there was horse racing, there were travelling circuses, puppet shows, singers, prostitutes (as many as three hundred at a time), magicians and fortune-tellers. There were also hundreds of incredibly glamorous soldiers stationed right there on the south coast, staring out at Boney across the English Channel: enough to drive Lydia Bennet wild. Jane Austen told her sister, in 1799, 'I assure you that I dread the idea of going to Brighton as much as you do, but I am not without hopes that something may happen to prevent it'; but her detestation of the place probably put her in the minority. What had once been little Brighthelmstone, a fishing village by the South Downs, was now a cynosure.

And then there was the Prince Regent. He had first come to Brighton (as mere Prince of Wales) in 1783, renting an almost modest house on the Steyne, in the middle of the seafront. Over the next thirty years, he made this his home from home, turning a quietly serviceable villa into the Royal Pavilion. Henry Holland produced the initial designs for something chaste and vaguely Italianate, but he was eventually thrown over in favour of the great John Nash – later, architect of Regent's Street in London. Between 1802 and 1822, the structure we know today achieved its final form: exotic, Indian style domes, towers and minarets outside; fanciful Indian-and Chinese-influenced decoration within . And of course the Prince filled it with his dodgy companions – the drunken playwright Sheridan, Beau Brummell, the alcoholic Duke of Norfolk, (Earl) Tommy Onslow – and dedicated himself to riotous drinking, eating, practical joking, gambling and sexual high-jinks. 'This wicked Pavilion', as one intimate called it, and it set a mood for Brighton, which nowhere else could match.

IX. Transport

Getting to Bath, Brighton, Scarborough, Godmersham, Tonbridge or Weymouth: that was the hard part. We are *just* on the brink of the railway age, with the Stockton and

Darlington line, the world's first public railway, opening to passengers in 1823. It would then be another seven or eight years to go before the railways could seriously challenge horse-drawn carriages and open roads. But until then, roads for fast travel, with canals for heavy goods, were the only options.

The good news was that, impelled by the need for a reasonably quick and reliable postal service, progress was being made on improving the road network. By the early 1820s, the ideas of Scottish civil engineers Thomas Telford, and then John McAdam, would see to it that smooth new highways could be built. When author Thomas De Quincy travelled with the high-speed mail coach, he was terribly excited, first by 'Velocity, at that time unprecedented', then by the way in which 'The connection of the mail with the state and the executive government gave to the whole mail establishment an official grandeur which did us service on the roads ... Look at those turnpike gates; with what deferential hurry, with what an obedient start, they fly open at our approach!'

The bad news was that, so far as Jane Austen and her contemporaries were concerned, the public roads, even those with turnpikes (whose tolls were used to repair and improve the highway) were still a mixed bag. The mail coach between Holyhead in Anglesey (North Wales) and Shrewsbury in Shropshire, for instance, was inaugurated in 1808 and closed again a few months later, on account of the terrible state of the Welsh roads. Lesser roads were barely kept up at all, and many were no more than rutted tracks, filled with potholes as much as five feet deep, only good for travel on horseback.

On the other hand, carriages that could run on the main roads were becoming uniformly lighter and fractionally more comfortable, with better suspensions and more appealing fixtures and fittings. Better yet, if you could afford to travel with the mail delivery coaches (it was a penny a mile extra on the fare), you not only enjoyed the latest, most refined technology, you also went express. The fast mail coaches, which had been running a special service for the Post Office since 1782, went to over three hundred different destinations, carried a limited number of passengers, were exempt from turnpike tolls, never travelled without an armed guard, changed their teams of horses at each stage within minutes rather than over a leisurely half-hour and could maintain an impressive average speed of eight miles an hour. Even regular stagecoaches – halting at intervals to change the teams of horses and allow the passengers time for refreshment – could carry as many as eight passengers on the inside and four outside (many travellers preferred to sit outside the coaches, on the roof, to escape the terrible fug which built up inside). They were also getting to the point where they could travel from Edinburgh to London in as little as forty hours. One visitor commented on 'The mechanical elegance and refinement' of the British stagecoach; while another was delighted by the coaching inns, with their 'Tubs of handsome porcelain, in which you may plunge half your body; cocks which instantly supply you with streams of water at Pleasure; half a dozen wide towels; a multitude of fine glass bottles and glasses, great and small; a large standing looking-glass, foot baths etc.'.

This was how Jane Austen got around England. We know that she nearly lost her trunk, her writings and her

'Worldly wealth' on one of the stages on the way to Godmersham; on another occasion 'We were late in London, from being a great load, and from changing coaches at Farnham; it was nearly four, I believe, when we reached Sloane Street'. And on another occasion:

> We had a very good journey, weather and roads excellent; the three first stages for 1s. 6d., and our only misadventure the being delayed about a quarter of an hour at Kingston for horses, and being obliged to put up with a pair belonging to a hackney coach and their coachman, which left no room on the barouche box for Lizzy, who was to have gone her last stage there as she did the first; consequently we were all four within, which was a little crowded.

Private transport was more exotic, unless one includes travelling by foot – the most common way to get around, and over long distances ('I had just left off writing and put on my things for walking to Alton, when Anna and her friend Harriot called in their way thither, so we went together'). Moonlit nights were naturally at a premium for the foot traveller. 'My father staid very contentedly till half-past nine (we went a little after eight),' Jane wrote of a ball at Lyme Regis, 'and then walked home with James and a lanthorn, though I believe the lanthorn was not lit, as the moon was up; but this lanthorn may sometimes be a great convenience to him.'

Sedan chairs – that halfway house between pedal locomotion and personal transport – were becoming increasingly rare. Bath still had a few, whose continued existence was sustained by the feebleness of the city's visitors; and in London, they were the only way a person of quality could be transported through the impossibly narrow lanes. Much smarter, was to ride a horse: but this meant that you had to be able to keep one in the first place (consider Mrs Dashwood's unease at the prospect of Marianne being given a horse by Willoughby) and be robust enough to put up with the ride. Jane Austen herself managed to ride a donkey in her last year; Mr Knightley doesn't keep a horse, even though he could clearly afford to; and much of the more daring riding is done by tearaways such as Henry Tilney, Edward Ferrars and Frank Churchill.

It is to Colonel Brandon's credit that he can ride as far as Honiton, before catching a more comfortable post-chaise – a smallish closed vehicle, usually for two people, capable of fast travel and one of the more common sights on the roads. The same was true of the wicked curricle, that sporting, two-wheeled, two-person carriage, drawn by a pair of horses and brazenly driven by a young man intending to impress a female companion. But the curricle, like the gig, or the rather sexier and classier four-wheel phaeton, was an uncompromising vehicle, with little or no weather protection, and an unsettled ride. What if one's position in society required something more civilized?

At this point, one enters the world of the private coach – a much grander, four-wheeled vehicle, capable of seating up to six passengers in something approaching comfort, and full of expressive dignity. 'The great expence of these carriages,' according to one Regency-era coachbuilder, thinking in particular of Continental travel, 'is principally on account of the many conveniences for luggage necessary for the passengers' accommodation.' But everything about these vehicles – from the graceful landaulet to the fabulously aristocratic barouche – cost money. The metalwork alone, brass buckles to iron wheel-hoops, could set you back £20 or more; while the owner's crest, painted on each side-door, was another £2. The Revd George Austen owned his own coach at the end of the eighteenth century, but was obliged to put it into storage on account of the costs of maintenance, which by now included taxation. So, when Lady Catherine de Bourgh refers to her barouche – big enough to carry three women passengers, 'If the weather should happen to be cool' – it is not just a piece of information about a carriage that she is vouchsafing; it is yet another reminder of her status.

X. After the Regency

Eventually, the democratic steam train would see off the barouche and the post-chaise, the Royal Mail would become even cheaper and more efficient, and English writer Sydney Smith would announce that 'Railroad travelling is a delightful improvement of human life. Man is become a bird; he can fly longer and quicker than a Solan Goose.' All of which was well and good, helping to liberate the energies of the nineteenth century; but also symptomatic of the transition from the settled, horse-drawn, communities of the early Regency, to the aggressively mobile, unsettled world of the Victorians. At the start of Jane Austen's life, more people lived in rural communities than in towns or cities. By the end of the Regency, that position had been reversed, and the restless urban age was upon us.

Nor did the end of the Napoleonic Wars bring much

peace. Rioting was a fact of life. There were the Luddite riots, starting in 1811 and continuing, on-and-off, for another four years; the food riots of 1816; the Peterloo Massacre of 1819. 'In the riots and meetings of those troublous time,' one commentator observed, 'the mob really meant mischief.' There was famine, chronic unemployment, deep misery at the way that life was corrupted by the exigencies of capitalism and the new industries. Soldiers and sailors who had fought across half of Europe found themselves discarded, living in poverty and searching for Poor Relief as a result. Children as young as ten years old toiled in the cotton mills. Until 1929, and the arrival of the Metropolitan Police, there was no centralized police force (even after 1929, the rest of the country still had to look after itself as best it could) but there were an awful lot of highwaymen, pickpockets, burglars and cutthroats: Harriet Smith's 'Trampers' in *Emma* – 'Half a dozen children, headed by a stout woman and a great boy' – being a fairly tame example of what was on offer. Popular politics were both rotten and violent too, with elections marked by more riots – especially in the neighbourhood of anyone known to be a Conservative: Princess Lieven (wife of the Russian ambassador to London) had to board up her house in Brighton during the election of 1820, and was afraid to go out of doors. It was a confused and angry time, only brightened by George IV's outrageous coronation (which cost nearly £250,000) at Westminster Abbey.

In a sense, Jane Austen, dying in 1817, had lived through the best of the Regency Era. Once the Regent had at last become King, he visited Ireland and Scotland (where he had himself glamorously depicted as a tartanned Highlander), before retreating to the security of Windsor Castle, from where he would rail against the emancipation of the Catholics. Hugely overweight, appallingly unhealthy and not entirely in his right mind, he slowly declined into death. He had failed to produce a living, legitimate, heir – his daughter Charlotte dying in the same year as Jane – and so the throne went to his duller, worthier, younger brother, William. As William IV, too, failed to produce a single legitimate heir – despite having produced a large family with the actor, Mrs Jordan – the crown was passed further down the line, to his niece, Princess Victoria.

And if there was anything left of the Regency by 1837, the energies of the Victorian age would soon overwhelm it.

4

AFTER JANE

Persuasion and *Northanger Abbey* emerged in print at the end of 1817, the year of Jane Austen's death, sold fairly well for a while, then disappeared from view. John Murray lost interest, and from 1820 to 1832, Miss Austen and her canon were out of print. By the mid-nineteenth century, the literary landscape had completely reordered itself: Charles Dickens, Anthony Trollope, William Thackeray, George Eliot and Wilkie Collins were at the heights of their respective powers, and the world fed on novels that were variously dark, satirical, troubled, grotesque, broadly hilarious, sinister, knotty and ambitious. Before too long, Herman Melville, Mark Twain and Edgar Allan Poe would have established a specifically American take on the modern novel, and the gigantic figures of Leo Tolstoy, Gustave Flaubert, Fyodor Dostoyevsky, Marie-Henri

Stendhal and Honoré de Balzac would be roaming the landscape of European literature. It was a bad time for the quiet certainties of *Emma* and *Mansfield Park*.

A publisher called Richard Bentley nevertheless took on Jane Austen's titles and reprinted them in 1832 as single (rather than three-part) editions, in his *Standard Novels* series. The year 1833 saw the first collected edition of the novels, and for a while they sold modestly to a small, rather connoisseurial, audience. Things only started to pick up when James Edward Austen-Leigh – one of Jane's nephews – produced his *Memoir of Jane Austen* in 1869. Stiff with High Victorian self-importance, the *Memoir* is pretty unreadable ('As my subject carries me back about a hundred years, it will afford occasions for observing many changes gradually effected in the manners and habits of society, which I may think it worth while to mention') as well as being slavishly protective of Miss Austen's reputation, with its constant nods to her 'Insight into character', her 'Love of children', her legitimate inclusion among those 'Who have approached nearest ... to the great master Shakespeare.' It also presents the world with an impossibly sentimentalized engraving of Miss Austen in the frontispiece, loosely based on Cassandra's take-it-or-leave-it watercolour sketch, but horribly frilled and sanitized, the basis for countless subsequent bowdlerized images.

On the other hand, it does her the inestimable service of quoting from her own letters – and these, with their candour, drollness, bracing self-mockery, become the corroborating evidence of her genius, proof that the books weren't an accident, but the product of a mind every bit as clever and funny as one would want it to be. And if it did

nothing else, it provided a focus in the second half of the
nineteenth century for those who, unlike Charlotte Brontë
(for whom Austen 'Ruffles her reader by nothing vehe-
ment, disturbs him with nothing profound'), had never
given up on the novels.

So in the next few decades, Jane Austen began her
reinvention from cult novelist to acknowledged literary great.
The process was driven forward both by the timeless artistic
merits of the novels and by the invisible personal presence of
their creator, freshly revealed as a miraculous combination of
seer, wit and self-effacing saint. Before long the critic George
Saintsbury had coined the term 'Janeite' to denote a person
obsessed with Jane Austen and her life, although his fondness
for the expression could not hide its undertow of prissy
cliquishness: something Virginia Woolf alludes to in her
description of 'Twenty-five elderly gentlemen living in the
neighbourhood of London who resent any slight upon her
genius as if it were an insult to the chastity of their Aunts'.
Henry James, a writer whose subtlety had something in
common with Jane's, admired her greatly (at the turn of the
century) but couldn't stop complaining about what he saw as
publishing hype, cynically elbowing her back into promi-
nence; or issuing waspish little approvals – her 'Light felicity',
her 'Narrow unconscious perfection of form', and her 'Little
master strokes of imagination' – which sound a bit like
detractions. Rudyard Kipling, on the other hand, showed his
approval by writing *The Janeites* (published 1916), a short
story about a confederacy of Austen-loving soldiers in the
chaos of the First World War whose shared love of Miss
Austen keeps them sane ('Every dam' thing about Jane is
remarkable to a pukka Janeite!').

The intelligentsia had started to claim her as their own special property; and literary criticism – which was by now a business in its own right – soon found itself making room for her as well. A. C. Bradley, a dauntingly prominent Shakespearian scholar, wrote favourably about her. In 1923, R. W. Chapman produced his definitive scholarly edition of the works. And in the late 1930s, Mary Lascelles produced *Jane Austen and Her Art* (1939), the first truly influential study of her writing. F. R. Leavis (in *The Great Tradition* of 1948) confirmed her centrality a decade later, declaring that she was one of a handful of novelists (George Eliot, Henry James and Joseph Conrad, the others) who promoted an 'Awareness of the possibilities of life'. Jane Austen is now considered *serious*: at the last count, the British Library lists over three hundred books on Jane Austen and her achievements.

What makes Austen unusual, of course, is the fact that she is not just respected academically, she is deeply popular with the reading public. She hasn't been out of print since the dark days of the first half of the nineteenth century; indeed, *Pride and Prejudice* has become one of those books that people reflexively place at the top of any list of favourite novels – as seen in a recent poll for World Book Day, 2007, in which *Pride and Prejudice* defeated *Lord of the Rings*, the Bible and *Great Expectations*, to earn itself the distinction of being known as Britain's best-loved book.

Part of her ongoing popularity has to do with the number of adaptations that her work has attracted. Nothing helps book sales like a film or TV adaptation, and there have been countless assaults on Miss Austen's prose over the decades – not without reason, given the opportunities an Austen novel generates for pretty actors, handsome leading men and good taste Regency settings. The first really big Austen movie was MGM's *Pride and Prejudice* of 1940, starring a somewhat matronly Greer Garson as Elizabeth Bennet, and Laurence Olivier on full smoulder as Mr Darcy. This was actually Jane Austen at several removes, based as it was on a stage version of the novel written by Helen Jerome, which was inflated to movie proportions by American screenwriter Jane Murfin and, of all people, Aldous Huxley (in 1940). 'Five love-hungry sisters', promises the trailer, and the dialogue takes it from there: 'It's much too nice just being alive, even if I never have a husband', announces Greer, before having an archery lesson with Mr Darcy, who calls her 'Darling' and kisses her full on the lips before they're even married. Miss Garson later claimed that the plainly anachronistic costumes were all recycled from *Gone With The Wind*, while Australian-born American Errol Flynn was at one stage tipped for the part of Darcy. As a consequence, most of the film's period charm has to do with the 1940s rather than the 1810s, but at least it set the ball rolling.

After the 1940 film release, scarcely a year went by without someone having a go: From *The Philco Television Playhouse* (*Pride and Prejudice*, 1949, and *Sense and Sensibility*, 1950), to *Matinee Theatre* (*Pride and Prejudice*, 1956, and *Emma*, 1957), to the *Kraft Television Theatre* (*Emma*, 1954), to *De Vier Dochters Bennet* (a Dutch TV version from the early 1960s), to *Orgoglio e Pregiudizio* (1957 Italian TV mini-series, starring the impossibly beautiful Virna Lisi), to *General Motors Presents* (*Pride and Prejudice*, 1958), to *La Abadía de Northanger* (Spanish, from 1968). Then, in 1952, the BBC, having already had a crack at *Emma*, turned *Pride and Prejudice* into a mini-series, with Peter Cushing (yes) as Darcy and Daphne Slater as Elizabeth Bennet. This turned out to be the first term in a series of Austen adaptations, whose relative fidelity to the original novels was evidently helped by stretching the action out over several episodes, and by having actors (Paul Daneman, Michael Gough, Patricia Routledge) who were reasonably familiar with period English. In fact the BBC has made itself more or less the default adapter of Jane Austen, doing *Pride and Prejudice* five times to date, *Emma* four times, *Persuasion* twice, *Sense and Sensibility* three times, *Northanger Abbey* once and *Mansfield Park* twice (if we include their involvement in the 1999 movie).

Not that the BBC can necessarily be trusted to play it completely straight – as is evidenced (at the very least) by Mr Darcy's completely inauthentic plunge into the lake, in the course of the 1995 *Pride and Prejudice* adaptation. The fact that an entire generation of female viewers went weak at the sight of a soaking wet Colin Firth emerging from the waters ('Mr Darcy!' 'Miss Bennet!') or that Firth smouldered broadly elsewhere in the series ('Dearest, loveliest Elizabeth') suggests that the BBC's curatorial relationship with the works of Jane Austen only goes so far before showbiz starts to count. Indeed, Firth became a real star only after adding his contribution to the lexicon of potent stares, tempestuous glances and manly heavings on which Regency dramatizations have come to depend. This in turn suggests that any dramatic interpretation of Miss Austen's prose is likely to be as much about mood as it is about language.

The 1995 film version of *Sense and Sensibility* feels more diligent in its approach to the Austen legacy. It's a clever balancing act from Emma Thompson, who wrote the script, and Ang Lee, who directed, but is let down by the fact that the novel itself is something of a mess. The scrambled final third of the book is fairly faithfully rendered in the corresponding scrambled third of the film, implying that if one is to tackle Austen at all, some other accommodation needs to be made to get the project to work. This means trying to have it both ways: treating Jane Austen's work with due respect, while making a watchable film.

There have also been a number of attempts to make movies out of the themes of the Austen novels, freshly treated. *I Have Found It* (2000) is a recent Indian take on *Sense and Sensibility*, and stars Aishwarya Rai Bachchan as Meenakshi, the Marianne Dashwood character, singing, 'Oh, chirping mynahs, on hearing my voice, flock together'. Some students at a University in Indiana took a contemporary run at *Sense and Sensibility* and came up with *Ellie and Marianne* ('Come on Ellie, don't be so boring!'); while *From Prada to Nada* (2011) does the same in a Latina context ('You clean up all right for a homeboy'); *Aisha* ([2010] 'Don't be cupid!') translates *Emma* to modern-day Delhi; *Clueless* (1995) moves *Emma* to Beverley Hills; and *Bride and Prejudice* (2004) – one of the more engaging re-imaginings – shifts the characters of Jane Austen's second published novel to Amritsar ('All mothers think that any single guy with big bucks must be shopping for a wife') turns them (almost) all into absurdly glamorous Indian actors, and has some fantastic song and dance sequences ('When the moon disappears, the light of your beauty takes its place'). The Merchant–Ivory team tried their luck with *Jane Austen in Manhattan* (1980), (two teachers squabble over who is going to produce a play written by Jane Austen when she was twelve); while *The Jane Austen Book Club* ([2007] from the novel of the same name) follows a group of latterday Janeites, whose lives begin to mirror the Austen novels they're reading ('All Jane Austen, all the time!').

Even more audaciously, one or two people have put Miss Austen *herself* in the movies. *Miss Austen Regrets* (a 2008 BBC/WGBH Boston co-production) pictures the middle-aged Jane attempting to find a suitable husband for her niece, Fanny Knight, while brooding on what might have been in her own life. Not only does Harris Bigg Wither make an appearance, but also Cassandra Austen, played (disorientingly enough) by one-time movie siren Greta Scacchi. And if that doesn't offer sufficient freewheeling licence with the details of Jane's biography, then try *Becoming Jane* (2007), in which a surprisingly luscious young Miss Austen (played by Anne Hathaway) quotes chunks of herself at an equally surprisingly feisty Tom Lefroy (played by James McAvoy) before hurling herself into his arms. Clearly, it has been open season on the Austen canon and all its related material for some time, and there is no sign of the process abating, nor of an outbreak of reticence when it comes to messing around with the facts.

And this is just film and TV. She has also been adapted for the stage, turned into musicals and granted a literary life beyond the grave. Quite apart from the novels which already exist in numerous editions,

translations and formats, there are scores of continuations –
zombie-like addenda to the originals – either, as in the case
of *Sanditon* and *The Watsons*, finishing off Miss Austen's
incomplete text, or taking existing characters and situations
and giving them a second, or third, narrative airing. Both
Emma Tennant and Joan Aiken have established alternative
careers as Austen-extenders; while writer Stephanie Barron
has gone so far as to turn Jane Austen into a detective in the
Jane Austen Mysteries series (1996–2006) – entangling her
with, among others, a Napoleonic spy, a corpse in the cellar
at Chawton, Lord Byron and 'The darkly forbidding yet
strangely attractive master of High Down Grange, Mr
Geoffrey Sidmouth.' (What is it with Jane Austen and
detective work, by the way, especially in the neighbourhood of Pemberley? A recent working-over – *Death
Comes to Pemberley* by the crime writer P. D. James
attracted a good deal of notice when it came out; but the
equally celebrated T. H. White also used Darcy's seat for a
kind of whodunnit, back in the 1930s, with his *Darkness at
Pemberley*. Dorothy Bonavia-Hunt's 1949 *Pemberley
Shades* did the same, only with a more Wilkie Collins/
Gothic spin.) There are also fictionalizations of Jane
Austen's own life (in the manner of *Miss Austen Regrets*) –
among them *Parson Austen's Daughter* (1949), *The Novelist, Jane, Our Own Particular Jane* (1975) and *Antipodes
Jane* ([1985] in which, yes, Miss Austen winds up in
Australia), all expressing the latent Janeite frustration that
there is just not enough Jane to go round, and that more, if
necessary, needs to be invented.

Leaving these thousands of pages of printed matter
behind, we then escape into the realms of purely human

interaction. The Jane Austen Society established itself in the UK in 1940, with the aim of saving Austen's house in Chawton. This was duly achieved by the Jane Austen Memorial Trust in 1947, leaving the Society to continue promoting Austen scholarship and curating her legacy – a job it still does, energetically, today. The English-speaking world of course has more than one Jane Austen Society: the United States has a startling number, with more in Canada, New Zealand, Australia, plus, at the time of writing, one in Argentina, and another in Brazil. And then there are the online resources, more than you can count, sharing, more or less reliably, information, reviews, bits of history, photographs, tittle-tattle, recipes for biscuits, Regency needlework patterns, opportunities to dress up in the Regency style, Regency dance tunes. At the same time, online sites allow thousands of worldwide Janeites (including German and Spanish speakers) to discuss matters of Janeite importance on Janeite forums, before, quite possibly, signing up for one of the many Jane Austen-related tours of Bath (and the rest of southern England) where one can then buy a Jane Austen T-shirt, selection of stationery, cookbook, lapel badge, bumper sticker, water-bottle . . .

Plenty of writers – from Shakespeare to Dan Brown – inspire degrees of idolatry. But the attention paid to Miss Austen, nearly two hundred years after her death, is hard to account for, however great a writer she was. She has become a brand in her own right: almost anything with 'Jane Austen' in the name now carries with it connotations of quality and good taste. Georgette Heyer was once a pretty fair writer of Regency novels (although, let's be frank, 1954's *The Toll-Gate* does start with the imperishable line 'The Sixth Earl of Saltash glanced round the immense dining-table, and was conscious of a glow of satisfaction'), but she was writing about an era which ended eighty years before she was born, and her literary reputation is now not much more than that of an entertaining *pasticheuse*. If Miss Heyer were writing now, her publisher would insist on getting Jane Austen's name onto the covers of her books, somehow, anyhow – a guarantee of value, or at least, a glimpse of the halo of authenticity which only Austen can bestow. More than that: as the unofficial Godmother of chick-lit (to use that marketing segmentation), with *Pride and Prejudice* the paradigm for all shrewd, ironical, but satisfyingly happy-ending romances, she has become the fixed reference point for a thousand latterday interpretations of the Elizabeth Bennet–Mr Darcy story; which, in turn, creates an obligation for all contemporary readers to go back and check the original version, if they haven't already done so. Her presence, in other words, extends beyond her novels into a larger fictional diaspora, and, as such is a marketing man's dream.

Why do people feel close to Miss Austen, even if they've barely read her? And what do they feel when something happens to injure, or merely affect, Jane's reputation? In 2007, a prankish (male) writer typed out the opening chapters of *Persuasion*, *Northanger Abbey* and *Pride and Prejudice* and sent them under a ladylike pseudonym to eighteen different UK publishers and agents, just to see how alert the industry was, how much of the nation's essential literary heritage it was actually familiar with. Seventeen out of the eighteen ignored Miss Austen's brilliance, turned it down, or simply didn't spot that it *was* Jane Austen – failing, even, to notice *Pride and Prejudice*. Only one publisher was awake enough to make the connection. This then turned into a scandal which made the national media – press and radio – and led to a week of noisy recrimination: that a national treasure such as Jane Austen could be treated so appallingly, as if someone had painted the British Museum pink.

On the other hand, when a new – possible – portrait of Miss Austen surfaced in 2011, it caused an even bigger stir. Drawn in graphite on vellum, bought at auction in the UK, owned by an Austen biographer and dated to some time early in the nineteenth century, the new image certainly *could* be of Jane Austen: the aquiline Austen nose is certainly prominent, and the eyes look about right, set in a slightly more mature face than the one familiar from Cassandra's sketch. And the figure is holding a pen and paper. More than that is, at the time of writing, unknown. Nevertheless, this find not only occasioned the main news on radio and TV (a bigger stir than the 2007 prank), it also made the front pages of the national press *and* generated a TV special, shown at prime time over the Christmas period, in the course of which various interested parties argued over the authenticity of the image. The (not entirely uniform) consensus of this programme suggested that it was a true likeness; although one had to wonder how much wishful thinking was involved. But who else could have commanded such devoted attentions? Other than Shakespeare? Could Sir Walter Scott have managed it?

The further we get from Jane Austen's world, the more we need it. Just as the Victorians – with their teeming cities, their steam trains and their relentless material progress – found themselves drawn to the pre-industrial verities of the novels, so we lose ourselves in a past which is ordered, moral, humanely sized and paced; and which is also absolutely contemporary in its sharpness, irony and want of unnecessary sentiment. If Miss Austen had known what kind of celebrity was waiting for her, two hundred years on, what would she have thought? Would she even have carried on writing? There are odd symmetries in the reticence of her life and writing, set against the inescapable fame they now enjoy. But they would not, in all probability, have been enough to persuade her that fame is an end in itself. Which is why we keep reading her.

BIBLIOGRAPHY

Auerbach, Emily, *Searching for Jane Austen* (University of Wisconsin Press, 2004).

Butler, Marilyn, *Jane Austen and the War of Ideas* (Clarendon Press, 1975).

Carson, Susannah (ed), *A Truth Universally Acknowledged* (Particular Books, 2010).

Chapman, R.W., *Jane Austen's Letters to her Sister Cassandra and Others* (Oxford University Press, 1952).

Craik, W.A., *Jane Austen in her Time* (Nelson, 1969).

Fergus, Jan, *Jane Austen and the Didactic Novel* (Macmillan, 1983).

Hardy, Barbara, *A Reading of Jane Austen* (Peter Owen, 1975).

Hodge, Jane Aiken, *The Double Life of Jane Austen* (Hodder & Stoughton, 1992).

Honan, Park, *Jane Austen: Her Life* (Weidenfeld & Nicolson, 1987).

Johnson, Claudia, *Jane Austen: Women, Politics and the Novel* (University of Chicago Press, 1988).

Lascelles, Mary, *Jane Austen and her Art* (Oxford University Press, 1941).

Low, Donald A., *That Sunny Dome* (Dent, 1977).

Murray, Venetia, *High Society: A Social History of the Regency Period 1788–1830* (Viking, 1998).

Pinion, F.B., *A Jane Austen Companion* (Macmillan, 1973).

Ross, Josephine, *Jane Austen: A Companion* (John Murray, 2002).

Sales, Roger, *Jane Austen and Representations of Regency England* (Routledge, 1994).

Southam, B.C., *Jane Austen: The Critical Heritage* (Routledge & Kegan Paul, 1968; 1987).

Spence, Jon, *Becoming Jane Austen* (Hambledon & London Press, 2003).

Tanner, Tony, *Jane Austen* (Macmillan, 1986).

Tannahill, Reay, *Food in History* (Penguin, 1988).

Tomalin, Claire, *Jane Austen: A Life* (Viking, 1997).

Waldron, Mary, *Jane Austen and the Fiction of her Time* (Cambridge University Press, 1999).

White, R.J., *Life in Regency England* (Batsford, 1963).

INDEX

alcohol 197–9, 200

Almack's Assembly Rooms 182–3

armed forces 3, 19, 137–8, 188–9, 215–16, 222

Assembly Balls, Basingstoke 9, 20, 206

Austen, Anna 50–1, 64, 66

Austen, Caroline 25–6, 33, 68, 73

Austen, Cassandra (sister) 4, 5, 8–9, 13, 14, 17, 21, 23–4, 26, 27, 33, 54, 72–6, 212, 231

   JA's letters after first publication 35, 41–2, 57–8, 67–8, 165–6, 179

   JA's letters before first publication 2, 3, 10, 11–12, 13, 14, 15, 16, 17, 20–3, 28–9, 30, 172, 214, 216

JA's letters of unspecified date 171, 180, 181, 191, 192, 197, 199

Austen, Charles (brother) 3, 137

Austen, Frank (brother) 3, 28, 29–30, 43, 45, 75, 188

Austen, George (brother) 3, 185

Austen, Henry (brother) 3, 7, 24, 34–5, 36, 45, 48, 55, 56, 66–7, 71, 73–4, 75, 189–90

Austen, James (brother) 3, 20, 24–5, 28, 30, 50, 53

Austen, Jane

   advises nieces 50–4

   appearance 9, 33, 235

   balls and social life 9, 14, 15, 16, 18, 19, 21–2, 32, 36, 202–3, 206, 207

and Bath 17–18, 20–3, 24, 28, 29
birth 2
book reviews 37–8, 42–3, 64–6, 78, 118–19
Chawton 29, 30–1, 32, 33–4, 39, 72, 163–4, 233
coach travel 14–15, 23, 211, 218–19
death and funeral 75
death of father 28
education 4, 180
food and drink 194–5, 196–7, 198–9, 200
games 202–3
health 4, 67–9, 72–5
ladies fashion 173
and London 17, 36, 45
in modern fiction 232
piano playing 4–5, 31, 39, 181, 182
popularity after death 224–36
and the Prince Regent 55–7, 66, 161
publishes *Emma* 55–6, 57, 59, 63–6
publishes *Mansfield Park* 48, 49, 119–20
publishes *Northanger Abbey* 143–4
publishes *Pride and Prejudice* 40–3
publishes *Sense and Sensibility* 34–6, 37–8
and Revd James Stanier Clarke 56, 58–61, 66
romantic interests 10–13, 20, 23–5

seaside resorts 214, 216
sewing 4, 14, 180, 182
and Sidmouth 213–14
and Southampton 29–30, 31
at work 39–40
see also Austen, Cassandra (sister); individual novels by name
Austen Knight, Edward (brother) 3, 14, 16–17, 28, 30–1, 34, 55, 67, 73, 74, 75
Austen Knight, Elizabeth 17, 28, 30, 35–6
Austen-Leigh, Cassandra (mother) 3, 13, 15, 17, 20, 23, 26, 31, 32, 33, 41, 190
Austen-Leigh, James Edward 2, 225
Austen, Revd George (father) 2–3, 4, 14, 15, 19, 20, 21, 26, 28, 190, 221

balls and social life 9, 14, 15, 16, 18, 19, 21–2, 32, 36, 182–3, 201–8, 215–16
Bath 16–18, 20–3, 24, 26, 28, 204, 212, 219–20
BBC (British Broadcasting Company) 229, 231
Bennet, Elizabeth 40, 43, 91, 92, 93, 175–6, 191, 204, 207, 209
see also Pride and Prejudice: storyline
Bentley, Richard 225
Bessborough, Lady 38, 78
Bigg Wither, Harris 24–5, 231

Bigg Wither, Lovelace 24
birth of JA 2
Blackall, Samuel 14
Bonaparte, Napoleon 159
Brighton 17, 214–16, 222
British Critic 37, 42–3, 64, 78
Brummell, Beau 176–8, 216
Burney, Fanny 26, 36–7

Cadell publishers 14
card games 202–4
Caroline, Princess of Brunswick
    158, 161
Chard, George 4–5
Charlotte, Princess 38, 78, 158, 223
Chawton (Austen home) 29, 30–1,
    32, 33–4, 39, 72, 163–4, 233
Clarke, Revd James Stanier 56,
    58–61, 66
clergymen, status of Regency 187
coach travel 217–19, 220–1
Cobbett, William: *Advice to
    Young Men* 185–6
cookery books 195
Cowper, William 15, 105
Craven, Lord 8–9, 13
Critical Review 37, 42, 78
Crosby & Co. publishers 32–3, 71
Crosby & Cox publishers 26, 144

dancing 204–8
Darcy, Mr 43, 91, 93, 169, 191,
    209, 210
    see also Pride and Prejudice:
    storyline
De Quincy, Thomas 217

death and funeral of JA 75
debutantes, Regency 183
dramatic adaptations of JA's work
    227–31
dress and fashion, Regency
    men's 176–9
    women's 172–6
drinks 197–200

Edgeworth, Maria 37, 46, 49, 143
education
    JA's 4, 179–80
    men and the Regency Era 183–6
    women and the Regency Era
    179–82
Egerton, Thomas 34–5, 47–8, 49
Elinor and Marianne (JA) 8, 14, 34
    see also Sense and Sensibility
Elliot, Anne 69, 70–1, 133, 134,
    136, 138
    see also Persuasion: storyline
Emma (JA) 55–6, 57, 59, 61–6,
    117–21, 167–8, 180, 182, 191,
    201, 206, 209–10, 222, 230
    storyline 121–32
etiquette 208–12

Farrer, Reginald 78, 119
fashion, Regency 172–9
Feuillide, Eliza, Comtesse de 5, 6,
    7, 24
finances
    George Austen (father) 3, 19
    Henry Austen 66–7
    JA's 26, 28–9, 30–1, 35, 39, 43,
    55, 74

First Impressions (JA) 8, 14, 16
food and drink, Regency 193–201
Fowle, Tom 8–9, 13, 24, 30
France 159–60

games, parlour 201–4
Gentleman's Magazine, The 64
George III, King 155, 213
George IV, King (earlier Prince
    Regent) 38, 55–7, 66, 155–9,
    161, 196, 214, 216, 222–3
Godmersham 14, 28, 30, 46–7,
    165–6, 168, 171–2
gothic novels 144–6

Hackett, Sarah (Mrs Latournelle) 4
health (JA's) 4, 67–9, 72–5
Heyer, Georgette 233–4
horse riding 220
households, Regency
    middle/upper class 162–7,
    169–70

internet resources 233

James, Henry 226
Jane Austen Society 233
Janeites 226, 233
Janeites, The (Rudyard Kipling)
    226
Juvenilia (JA) 5–7, 144

Kipling, Rudyard 226
Knight, Fanny 47, 51–5, 72–3, 75,
    207, 231

Lady Susan (JA) 7–8
landscape gardens 168–9
Lefroy, Anna 10, 11, 12, 33, 181
Lefroy, Fanny 24, 31–2
Lefroy, Louisa 24
Lefroy, Tom 10–13, 231
Lesley Castle (JA) 5–6
letter writing, Regency 192–3
    see also under Austen,
        Cassandra (sister)
lifestyle, Regency middle / upper
    class 163–70
lighting in homes 170–1
literature, nineteenth century
    post-Regency 224–5
Lloyd, Martha 19, 31, 161
Lloyd, Mary 31, 53, 75
Love and Friendship (JA) 6–7
Lymington, Lord 4

manners 208–12
Mansfield Park (JA) 43, 47,
    48–9, 55, 58, 102–3, 119–20,
    204
    storyline 104–17
meals 193–201
Memoir of Jane Austen (J. E.
    Austen-Leigh) 225–6
Monthly Review 64
Morland, Catherine 145, 146, 148,
    149
    see also Northanger Abbey:
    storyline
Murray, John 49, 55, 57–8, 64–5,
    119–20, 224

Napoleonic Wars 67, 137, 159–60, 193–4
Nash, Beau 17, 204
Nash, John 156, 216
Navy, Royal 3, 19, 137–8, 188, 189
New Review 42
Northanger Abbey (JA) 14, 16, 18, 26, 32, 35, 71–2, 76, 143–8, 204, 206, 224
   storyline 149–54

Pasley, Captain Charles William 42, 43
Perrot, James Leigh 17–18, 67, 73
Perrot, Jane Leigh 18, 20, 73
Persuasion (JA) 69–71, 76, 132–9, 214, 224
   storyline 139–43
piano playing 4–5, 31, 39, 181, 182
Plan of a Novel (JA) 61–2
Plumtree, John 51–3
Price, Fanny 48, 103, 104
   see also *Mansfield Park:* storyline
Pride and Prejudice (JA) 8, 39, 40–6, 91–3, 181, 191, 204, 227, 228, 229, 234
   storyline 93
professions, Regency 186–90
public school, Regency 184
publishers 14, 26, 32–3, 34–5, 47–8, 49, 55, 64–5, 224, 225

Quarterly Review 65–6

Regency Era
   alcohol 197–9, 200
   armed forces 3, 19, 188–9, 215–16, 222
   clergymen 187
   dancing 204–8
   debutantes 182–3
   food and drink 193–201
   games 201–4
   historical overview 155–61
   homes and households 162–7, 169–71
   landscape gardens 168–9
   manners 208–12
   men's daytime pursuits and professions 186–90
   men's dress and fashion 176–9
   men's education and accomplishments 183–6
   post-dinner entertainment 201–7
   sea-bathing and seaside resorts 212–16
   transport 216–21
   travel 212–16
   women's daytime pursuits 190–3
   women's dress and fashion 172–6
   women's education and accomplishments 179–82
Regent, Prince (later George IV) 38, 55–7, 66, 155–9, 161, 196, 214, 216, 222–3
Repton, Humphrey 168–9
reviews (JA's), book 37–8, 42–3, 64–6, 78

Richardson, Samuel 5
rioting in Britain 222
roads, public 217
Royal Navy 3, 19, 137–8, 188, 189

Saintsbury, George 226
Sanditon (JA) 72
Scott, Sir Walter 64–6, 118–19
seaside resorts 213–16
sedan chairs 74, 219
Sense and Sensibility (JA) 8, 14,
    34–9, 43, 55, 77–9, 181–2, 201,
    230
  storyline 79–91
servants 164–5, 166
sewing 4, 14, 180–1, 182
Sidmouth, Devon 213–14
Southampton (Austen home)
    29–30, 31
Steventon (Austen home) 2–3,
    13–14, 18, 20, 21, 24, 30, 164
Susan
  see *Northanger Abbey*

tea 199–200
transport, Regency 216–21
travel destinations, Regency
    212–16

United States of America 160
universities, Regency 184–5, 186
Upper Assembly Rooms, Bath
    204–5

Victoria, Queen 223

Walter, Philadelphia 5
Watsons, The (JA) 26–7
Which Is The Heroine? (Anna
    Austen) 50–1
William IV, King 158, 223
Winchester Cathedral 75, 76
women novelists, status of 36–7
Woodhouse, Emma 62–3, 118,
    120, 181–2, 201–2, 209–10
  see also *Emma:* storyline
Woolf, Virginia 119, 135, 141, 226